BACKROADS & BYWAYS OF

MONTANA

BACKROADS & BYWAYS OF
MONTANA

Drives, Day Trips
& Weekend Excursions

Jeff Welsch and
Sherry L. Moore

The Countryman Press
Woodstock, Vermont

We welcome your comments and suggestions.

Please contact

Editor
The Countryman Press
P.O. Box 748
Woodstock, VT 05091

or e-mail countrymanpress@wwnorton.com.

Backroads & Byways of Montana
ISBN 978-0-88150-899-4

Book design by Hespenheide Design
Map by Erin Greb Cartography, © The Countryman Press
Interior photos by the author unless otherwise specified
Composition by Chelsea Cloeter

Published by The Countryman Press, P.O. Box 748, Woodstock, VT 05091

Distributed by W. W. Norton & Company, Inc., 500 Fifth Avenue, New York, NY 10110

Printed in the United States of America

10 9 8 7 6 5 4 3 2 1

How This Book Works

This is a book about the best driving tours in Montana. It's also about capturing Montana's essence through 11 drives, each revealing a different portrait of the Treasure State's wide range of landscapes, communities, and personalities.

Our routes are all over the Montana map, literally and figuratively. Some are obvious, such as the dramatic Going-to-the-Sun Road in Glacier National Park and the Beartooth All-American Highway between Red Lodge and Cooke City. Some are included for the culture, such as the Big Sky Backcountry Byway in eastern Montana. Some are on well-maintained paved roads; some are on gravel or dirt that could be impassable after a rain- or snowstorm.

At the beginning of each chapter, you'll get the basics about the designated drive—where it starts, mileage, estimated time, highlights, and how to get there. You'll also get an overview of the area and its significance to Montana's history, geography, and culture. We then complement the chapters with a short story about a relevant topic, a composite weekend itinerary in case your time is short, and the best bars on the route. And at the end, assuming the tour has whet your appetite for more, we add one for the road—a nearby detour with its own brand of character and charm. To give you a sense of just how rural Montana is—and, in many cases, to temper expectations for services—we've included the populations for each community our routes traverse.

For consistency's sake, each route starts from a point or points on or near I-90, the heavily traveled freeway bisecting the state east to west. We chose to start each drive in a community where essential amenities are available. Of course, in many cases you'll be coming from a different direction and can plan your drives accordingly; we chose what we believe to be the most likely starting point for most visitors.

We feature attractions, scenery, points of interest, lodging, and dining that best tell the tour's story. Because driving in Montana frequently requires an overnight bag, we've also included Best Places to Bunk. For the 11 primary routes, we have listed a cost guide for dining and lodging (dining based on the average price of a dinner entrée). We also offer insights into signature menu items and try to note whether eateries are open for breakfast, lunch, and/or dinner. Hours can vary significantly between seasons, days, and sometimes even the whims of staffs, so call ahead—or take your chances as part of the adventure. Our lodging and dining price guide is as follows:

Lodging	*Dining*
$: $75 and under	$: $10 or less
$$: $76–125	$$: $11–20
$$$: $126–199	$$$: $21–30
$$$$: $200 and over	$$$$: $30 and over

These routes are mostly rural and often have limited restaurant options. Most places in Montana pride themselves on their burgers; this phenomenon could itself be a guidebook. From Alzada to Zortman, we ate dozens of great brawny, juicy, handmade hamburgers—some with secret ingredients. Though a few restaurants are known for their culinary skills, this isn't a fine-dining guide. Eateries were chosen for many reasons—sometimes quality, sometimes quirkiness, sometimes location, and sometimes because it was the only choice.

Lodging options included in this book reflect similar diversity. We have covered upscale accommodations as well as motor-court motels for those on a budget or looking for a more authentic experience. We have also added a category called Alternative Bunking for anyone driving an RV, camping, or wanting to have a one-of-a-kind experience in a Forest Service lookout or cabin (reservations: 877-444-6777 or www.recreation.gov). Much of Montana has wonderful dude and guest ranches; we omitted many appealing all-inclusive places simply because the concept of staying in one place for a week doesn't jibe with driving our routes.

Both lodging and dining listings should be open year-round unless otherwise noted.

Montana is famous for its ubiquitous bars and saloons, so we give them a nod, too, in a category called Best Bars. Though all bars are unique in their own right, we have highlighted a select one or two for each route based on their history, character, food options (in most cases), and the overall vibe we felt when stopping for a drink and conversation with locals and visitors.

Montana is a vast state. We recognize that time is often short, and you won't be able to explore everything we cover in these routes. Thus we've included a section called Perfect Weekend—the sites we would choose to see and the places we would dine and stay if time is limited. The general assumption is that these routes will be driven in summer, the most popular time, and again, if places are not open year-round, we've tried to note accordingly. A word to the wise: A good many rural establishments in Montana only accept cash.

One other note: you'll notice frequent references to the seven Indian reservations that help give Montana much of its character. Throughout the book, we refer to the people who live on these small remnants of their historical territories as "Indians" instead of "Native Americans." From our experiences in the region, this is their preference, and we have made every effort to honor it.

To fully absorb the flavor of this state of treasures and appreciate what you're about to experience, we encourage you to first read the introduction and following chapter on Montana's wide-ranging geography, history, and culture. This should provide ample background for the memorable journeys you're about to undertake.

Happy trails!

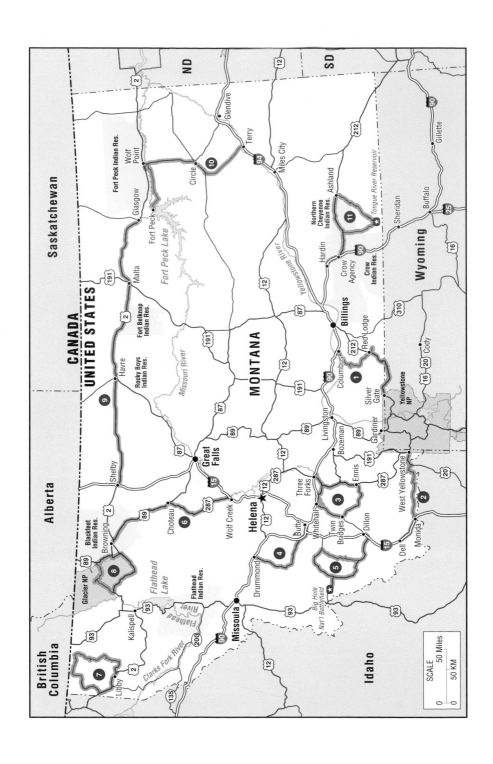

Contents

Introduction

Think Montana, and images of snowcapped mountains, pristine rivers, and weathered cowboys traversing vast prairies astride proud horses likely come to mind. After all, these portraits are the core of the Montana mystique, captured in the lilting prose of Ivan Doig and A. B. "Bud" Guthrie, the vivid paintings of C. M. Russell, and the breathtaking cinematography in *A River Runs Through It, The Horse Whisperer,* and *Legends of the Fall.*

Certainly, this is the romanticized Montana, and yet these snapshots offer an inspiring dose of accuracy as well. Even today, more than a century after the open-range era that emblazoned the Old West's image in the American psyche, visitors can participate in an actual cattle drive, cast a caddis or nymph to glistening pools teeming with fat wild trout, and marvel at brawny mountains in every direction. In many respects, Montana is still a raw, rugged, and wild place—even as well-heeled faux cowboys from the outside world flood river valleys and mountain resorts in the western half of the state. In reality, they are lured by a yearning to reconnect to a bygone era that's probably more myth than truth.

Yet it's still possible to experience the Montana of yesteryear, especially if you're willing to leave behind the well-traveled highways that serve the whims of tourists and newcomers. It's on these back roads and byways where the adventurous can see why Guthrie dubbed Montana the Big Sky Country. You'll readily appreciate the new definition of the old moniker

"Treasure State": After referring for a century to its rich reserves of minerals, timber, rangelands, and fossil fuels, the nickname now describes Montana's scenic, cultural, and natural wonders.

Once away from the hum of Missoula, Kalispell, Billings, Great Falls, and Bozeman—still small by eastern standards but veritable metropolises in a state that had yet to surpass 1 million residents in 2010—you'll find a remarkable variety of landscapes and peoples.

Did you know, for instance, that Montana has a temperate rain forest? The hardy, rugged loggers and farmers of the cool, damp, and gray Yaak River Valley in the northwest corner certainly can tell you about it.

Did you know that the state is dotted with semiarid deserts? Lest you doubt, check with the ranchers near Bridger in the south-central part of the state and Hot Springs in the northwest, where annual rainfalls in a good year are about the same as in Tucson, Arizona.

Did you know that a state famed for rivers also features the largest freshwater lake in the western United States? Cherry and grape growers—yes, frigid Montana even has a few wineries—are forever grateful for the fertile soils and moderate climes around Flathead Lake, one of the purest bodies of water of such scope and size in the world.

Did you know that Montana has seven Indian reservations, all on the same wide-open spaces—albeit a fraction of their historical lands—where the indigenous peoples once hunted bison and fished for native cutthroat trout? Drive across the reservation lands of the Crow, Northern Cheyenne, Blackfeet, Cree, Assiniboine, Sioux, and others, and it won't require much imagination to envision Indians on horseback atop a coulee, silhouetted against a cobalt sky.

With a state so huge and diverse, it's a challenging task to pare down a list of compelling back roads and byways to a mere handful. After all, at 147,000 square miles, Montana is surpassed in size only by Alaska, Texas, and California. It's at least an 11-hour drive across the state from east to west, and that's with your mettle fully on a 75-mph pedal on I-90.

In *Backroads & Byways of Montana,* we have detailed a collection of memorable drives that reflect the many geographic, historical, and social faces of Montana.

You'll meander amid towering fir and spruce in the foggy shadows of the northwest corner. You'll touch the stars atop the broad shoulders of the Beartooth Highway, once dubbed by CBS newsman Charles Kuralt as the most beautiful road in America. You'll be smitten with the untamed Rocky

Mountain Front, where grizzly bears can still be seen on the prairie.

You'll step back 150 years to the unspoiled Centennial Valley, a critical Greater Yellowstone Ecosystem migration route for such iconic wildlife species as wolves, grizzly bears, wolverine, moose, and elk. You'll watch the sun set beyond the Bitterroot in the upper Big Hole Valley, where you may hear the wailing ghosts of Nez Perce mourning a futile pursuit of freedom. You'll wind your way past waterfalls, mountain goats, and breathtaking vistas up…and up…and up…toward the sun, all the while gazing in awe at the incomparable beauty of Glacier National Park.

You'll discover where to enjoy the best eats, whether it's savoring sometimes-local beef, bison, or lamb under the watchful eyes of trophy elk mounts in darkened saloons or it's harder-to-find vegetarian fare in eclectic settings. You'll find out where to draw a draft of locally produced microbrews or traditional domestic lager while gazing at century-old back bars hauled up the Missouri on steamships. You'll have choices of lodging ranging from primitive to cowboy luxe. And along the way you'll find out about things to do and see and how to enjoy the many faces of Montana's attractions.

Oh, and we'll throw in a few trout streams and mountains along the way, too.

A Montana Primer:
History, Geography, and Driving

In our ethnocentric world, the calendar shows Montana's birth date as November 8, 1889, when after 25 years as a territory the state was welcomed into the union by proclamation of President Benjamin Harrison. The truth, of course, is that the scenic, cultural, and spiritual wonders of Montana really began to take shape about 100 million years ago, when the Rocky Mountains were born and converted what had been shallow seas, swamps, and plains into the dramatic geography we see today.

Anyone familiar with the fiery turbulence just beneath the earth's surface at Yellowstone National Park understands the violent genesis of the region. The Yellowstone supervolcano has erupted three times in the past 2.2 million years—the last about 700,000 years ago. They were the most dramatic forces during a period in which molten rock pushed upward in what is now western Montana, creating the mountain ranges for which the state is named and famed. Their mostly north–south direction can be attributed to tectonic plates grinding, folding, and thrusting from the west, pinching the land so that it was forced upward rapidly along faults. Over time, wind, rain, snow, and ice have eroded the mountains and carved deep river valleys.

The first significant life forms were the dinosaurs that roamed the swamps and plains about 150 million years ago, before the Rockies were formed. Fossilized bones and eggs have been found everywhere east of the mountains, from Choteau on the Rocky Mountain Front to the small canyons and plains of eastern Montana. To paleontologists, Montana is a geological treasure trove, and the distant presence of dinosaurs has created a bounty reflected in museums across the state. Energy companies also covet the dinosaur legacy. Oil, gas, and coal are abundant beneath the surface where the mountains meet the plains, and the countryside is sprinkled with oil and gas wells all the way to North Dakota.

As far as historians can tell, the first humans came to present-day Montana from what is now Russia during the last Ice Age, which ended approximately 11,000 years ago. They hunted the woolly mammoth and avoided the saber-toothed cat for several thousand years after the glaciers retreated, eventually dispersing when the land became too arid to provide enough game for subsistence. Shortly after, another group of tribes arrived, this time from the west and south. They, too, eventually disappeared, leaving a human void that wasn't filled until about 1,000 years ago.

History

A common misperception is that such Montana tribes as the Sioux, Assiniboine, Crow, Northern Cheyenne, Blackfeet, Flathead, Kootenai, Kalispell, Gros Ventre, Arapaho, and Nez Perce roamed the plains and mountains unfettered for thousands of years, their worlds abruptly shattered by migrating white settlers in the 1800s. Truth is, their heyday probably lasted about 250 years, from the time the Flatheads arrived around 1500 until they were banished to reservations by the 20th century. The earliest evidence of modern-day tribes is the Crows, dating to about 1150. The Sioux, pushed west by the advancing Europeans, sought refuge on the inhospitable plains of the Dakotas and eastern Montana before they were subdued by the relentless white expansion.

French fur traders began trickling into the region as early as the 1740s, but the defining moment of the European invasion was the 1804–06 Lewis and Clark expedition that began in St. Louis, Missouri, and crossed Montana east to west en route to Fort Clatsop, Oregon. Some of the most memorable reports from the expedition occurred along the Missouri and Yellowstone rivers in what is now Montana. Ironically, the expedition was probably saved from disaster by a native woman named Sacagawea, who guided the group across the imposing Bitterroot Mountains along the backbone of the Rockies in the winter of 1805. The single remaining visible evidence of the corps is preserved under glass on a small sandstone butte called Pompey's Pillar, along the Yellowstone east of Billings. There, Captain William Clark etched his name and the date he camped there amid the cottonwoods; the butte is named for Sacagawea's son.

The Lewis and Clark trek eventually brought a flood of immigrants, most of them homesteaders with visions of wide-open spaces where they could raise crops amid lush shoulder-high prairie grasses and get rich from gold nuggets gleaming in the rivers. Reality was quite different. Cattle eventually grazed the grass to nubs, turning prairies into dusty lands ripe for invasive plants. Homesteaders suffered through long winters and dry summers, causing many to abandon dreams and leave their sod houses. The frontier Montana epitomized by the so-called open-range era of cattle ranching was short-lived as well. This mystical time began in 1866 when Nelson Story drove a herd from Texas to Montana on the Bozeman Trail—the film *Lonesome Dove* was based on this journey—leading the way for others to follow. The open-range era lasted about two decades, effectively ending during the brutal winter of 1886–87 in which half the state's cattle perished due to the lethal combination of overgrazed lands and wicked blizzards.

The mining boom in the southwest part of Montana Territory was fleeting as well. Gold was discovered in a mountain creek near Helena in 1858, and subsequent finds over the next few years brought men with picks and shovels by the thousands. Silver and copper were also unearthed. Such towns as Virginia City, Nevada City, Bannack, Garnet, Granite, Coolidge, Southern Cross, and Elkhorn rose from the piney hillsides overnight and became tawdry centers of drinking, carousing, and lawlessness. When the mines played out, the miners departed; the ghostly remnants of many of those towns still stand as an eerie testimony to a rags-to-riches-to-rags legacy.

Two other migrations are significant in Montana's pre-1900 history: missionaries and the railroads. In the 1830s, Jesuit priests reputedly were invited by native tribes for spiritual instruction, though many historians suspect the Indians were looking for more tangible items such as guns, food, and medicine. In any event, many missions are scattered on tribal lands throughout Montana, including St. Mary's near Stevensville south of Missoula, St. Ignatius on the Flathead Indian Reservation of northwest Montana, and St. Xavier on the Crow Indian Reservation southeast of Billings. The first railroad didn't arrive until 1880, the Utah & Northern. Three years later, the Northern Pacific became Montana's first transcontinental line. Spurs were built, and cattle towns sprang up much like gold towns. The ability to ship cattle to the Midwest, East, and South created vast wealth for cattle barons.

Life still isn't easy in Montana. Winters are long and cold even as the climate warms discernibly. Until the 1990s, the economy ebbed and flowed on the wildly fluctuating values of natural resources. Every boom, whether the gold rush of the 1860s or the energy frenzy after 9/11, has ended with a bust—or at least a palpable leveling off. Today, Montana is cashing in on another natural resource: its natural beauty and wildness. With the increasingly frenetic pace of life on both coasts and metropolitan areas, Montana has become a destination for people seeking new lives because it's one of the few remaining places in the country where vestiges of yesteryear remain.

Geography

Not surprisingly, given its size, Montana is a state of many distinct regions. In general, residents divide the state into two halves: western Montana, with its rugged mountains and cool rushing rivers, and eastern Montana, known for its plains, canyons, and warm meandering streams.

Within that division are six more regions, largely created by the state's tourism bureau but nonetheless relevant. Some are the size of small eastern states, and all are composed of subregions worthy of their own names.

Yellowstone Country of southwest Montana features the burly mountain ranges and pristine trout streams of travel brochures and famously includes the 3 percent of Yellowstone National Park in Montana. The Beartooth Highway and Centennial Valley drives are *Backroads & Byways of Montana* routes in this region.

Glacier Country of northwest Montana tends to include the most densely forested areas of the state, highlighted by the jagged peaks and jewel-like lakes of Glacier National Park. This area features the Going-to-the-Sun Road and Yaak River Country tour.

Gold Country of western Montana offers forests, broad picturesque valleys, and the remnants of once-flourishing mining and logging economies. Included are the Anaconda-Pintler Scenic Route, the Vigilante Trail, and Big Hole Valley driving route.

Russell Country is largely characterized by undulating prairies rising gently to abrupt meetings with walls of mountains, most strikingly on display at the confluence of the plains and vast Bob Marshall Wilderness. The Rocky Mountain Front is a highlight of this country.

Mailboxes along the rural route near Red Lodge. John Baker

Missouri River Country is Montana's windswept northeastern corner and features mile after mile of wheat fields, farms, and the Missouri River Breaks. The Hi-Line bisects this part of Montana as well as Russell Country, and the Big Sky Backcountry Byway enters this area, too.

Custer Country is marked by the wide-open spaces of southeastern Montana, where the term *big sky* comes to vivid life amid coulees, prairies, sunsets, and Montana's most famous Indian country. The Warrior Trail covers a corner of Custer Country.

Driving in Montana

As much as anywhere in America, it's imperative to be prepared when driving in Montana. In winter, Montanans know never to drive anywhere without having the equipment to spend a night on the side of the road. That includes matches, candles, water, sleeping bags, blankets, boots, gloves, and plenty of warm clothes. With a warming climate, winters aren't as harsh as the old-timers remember them, but 20 to 30 degrees below zero

Deep snows make plowing the Beartooth Highway a lengthy chore in May.
Montana Dept. of Transportation

isn't uncommon. Winds whip across the plains and down mountainsides, creating blinding conditions in a heartbeat. The Rocky Mountain Front, from Browning in the north to Livingston in the south, is renowned for its winter Chinooks, serving up wind speeds of up to 70 mph and scouring the valleys of snow. Even the most beautiful autumn or spring day can turn on a dime; it has snowed in every month in Montana, and snowstorms in June and September are not aberrations.

If you want some weather certainty, plan your vacation between late June and late September. A typical summer day in much of Montana begins with blue skies in the morning, some afternoon clouds, an isolated thunderstorm or two around dusk, and then evening clearing. Even summer provides its challenges, though. Traffic can be heavy, with campers and motor homes clogging roads.

An old joke is that there are two seasons in Montana: winter and road construction. Patience is a requirement, even in these wide-open spaces. Late-afternoon thunderstorms are common in the summer, rapidly turning a dirt or gravel road into impassable gumbo. If you're on a remote gravel road, you can easily get stuck. With its dry air, Montana's 90-degree days become 45-degree nights. It's no surprise that the most precipitous temperature plunge in 24 hours in U.S. history—100 degrees—took place in Montana in 1916, at Browning on the Blackfeet Indian Reservation. Equally dramatic was the 84-degree drop in 12 hours at Fairfield in 1924.

In the old days, Montana was so big, broad, and lightly trafficked that many highways didn't require speed limits. "Reasonable and proper" was the rule. Today, all roads have speed limits, topped by the 75 mph on the three interstate highways; two-lane rural state and county highways are 60 to 70. With these speeds and the monotonous countryside, be wary, especially at night. Drunken-driving and fatigue-related fatalities are categories where Montana has dubiously high rankings nationally.

Once upon a time, watching your fuel gauge was critical in Montana because distances between towns are great and many stations close after dark. Paying at the pump with credit cards has improved this situation, but many of the roads featured in this book have 60, 70, 80, or more miles between stations. Montana's fuel costs typically are average or a little below average compared to the rest of the country. Speaking of costs, Montana is one of five states that doesn't charge a sales tax, so it's a great place to buy that log bed or antler chandelier you've always wanted.

Breathtaking beauty greets drivers at every twisty turn on the Beartooth Highway.

CHAPTER

1

Highway to the Sky: The Beartooth Pass

Columbus to Silver Gate

Estimated length: 131 miles
Estimated time: 4 hours to 2 days (open June–Oct.)

Highlights: Scenic vistas, wildlife viewing, hiking, skiing, Top of the World Store, Yellowstone National Park's northeast entrance, mining history in Cooke City and Red Lodge.

Getting there: The Beartooth All-American Road typically is either the kickoff or exclamation mark for a Yellowstone National Park trip. For the kickoff, exit I-90 at Columbus. For the exclamation mark, folks leave Yellowstone through the northeast entrance after driving through the wildlife-rich Lamar Valley. The closest airports served by major airlines are in Bozeman and Billings, Montana, and Cody, Wyoming. To come through Yellowstone, leave I-90 at Livingston and drive 50 miles south through the aptly named Paradise Valley on US 89 to Yellowstone's north entrance at Gardiner. From there, it's 51 memorable miles through the park to Silver Gate. If you do happen to come from Cody, the drive over Chief Joseph Pass through Sunlight Basin on WY 296 to the junction of US 212 is one of the best-kept semi-secrets in Greater Yellowstone.

Overview

It has been several decades since the Beartooth was dubbed America's most beautiful drive. You'll quickly see why on a twisting ribbon of pavement

An aerial view of the Beartooth Highway's switchbacks south of Red Lodge
Montana Dept. of Transportation

that has the distinction of being the highest road in the Northern Rockies. The Beartooth All-American Road quickly rises from the vibrant old mining town of Red Lodge to almost 11,000 feet—less than 2,000 feet below the summit of nearby Granite Peak, the highest point in Montana. For context, the apex of the breathtaking Going-to-the-Sun Road in Glacier National Park is a paltry 6,646 feet.

Once on top, US 212 levels onto a broad alpine-tundra plateau known as the Beartooth Corridor, where the clouds seem close enough to pluck from the sky. Some 20 peaks of more than 12,000 feet are nearby, and the landscape is littered with glacial lakes that shimmer like jewels. Mountain goats and elk are common, and an occasional grizzly bear is spotted in the distance—a good reason to bring binoculars or a spotting scope. The elevation is so high that the road is typically only open from the Friday before

Memorial Day to the Tuesday after Columbus Day; the remainder of the year it's covered in snow. Frequent avalanches make plowing a proposition too futile or dangerous.

At first glance, you might wonder what would move anyone to build such a challenging highway. The short answer: The road was seen as a way to boost Red Lodge's economy in the Great Depression and create access to the potentially lucrative New World Mining District just northeast of Cooke City. The gold mining never panned out, but the road has been a boon to Red Lodge. The town has effectively marketed itself as a destination reminiscent of a younger Park City, Utah, and is a vibrant stopover for Harley riders, skiers, and anyone who appreciates combining a day in the great outdoors with an energetic nightlife.

About one-third of this drive is in Wyoming. But Montana has never been shy about claiming Yellowstone as its own even though only 3 percent of the park is within the state's boundaries, so why not the Beartooth All-American Highway as well? Further, the only way to reach Cooke City and Silver Gate is by passing in and out of Wyoming, making these two of the most remote outposts in Montana. The drive ends amid the spruce and firs of Silver Gate, a mile outside the northeast—and least-traveled—entrance to Yellowstone.

Even so, there is much more to this drive than the dramatic mountain vistas. The rolling pine, sage, and grass country between Columbus and Red Lodge is beautiful in its own right, and the Beartooths are always there with their spectacular and ever-closer backdrop. The communities along the way—Absarokee, Fishtail, Roscoe, Luther, and Red Lodge—are as inviting as any back-to-back collection of rural towns in Montana.

Hitting the Road

Columbus (pop. 2,039) sits in a pretty pine-studded bowl along the Yellowstone River, a blue-collar town with a smelter and refinery that seem to belie the setting. It's a fine place to gas up off the interstate, but there isn't much to see here. The free **Museum of the Beartooths** (406-322-4588, May–Sept.) offers a glimpse at the region's mining and homesteading history. **Montana Silversmith** (800-634-4830) is home to finely crafted jewelry for women and glossy western belt buckles for real and wannabe cowboys.

As you leave Columbus on MT 78 and follow the Stillwater River toward the Beartooths, look for some of the region's prettier barns and for

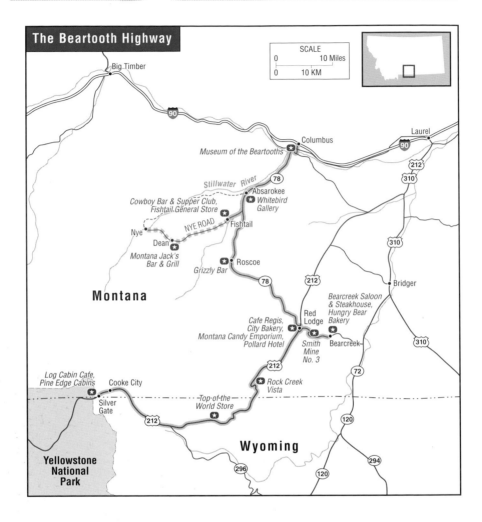

The Beartooth Highway

colorful flotillas of rafts plying the frothy river during spring and summer. The Stillwater is one of southwest Montana's favorite whitewater streams because of a relatively lengthy season. Guided full- and half-day raft trips along with fly-fishing excursions—the fishing is excellent, too—can be arranged with **Absarokee River Adventures** (800-334-7238), which also rents rafts and inflatable kayaks for do-it-yourselfers. To see the country on a mount, call Wanda at **Paintbrush Adventures** (406-328-4158) and arrange a one-hour or full-day ride or weeklong pack trip into Beartooth country. The Paintbrush hosts also provide guided day hikes and fishing trips, and for a true taste of western life, you can sign up for a working vacation on the ranch.

Twelve miles into the hill country is the cheerful community of **Absarokee** (pop. 1,300)—pronounced ab-SOHR-kee. Central to the town is **Big Yellow House** (406-328-7220), a registered historic home amid leafy trees that has the curious combination of seasonal lodging, a café, antiques, and Asian imports; the property was for sale in 2010 (the proprietor married and was moving to Kansas) so its future was uncertain. For a taste of local art, the **Whitebird Gallery** (406-328-7777) showcases some of Montana's finest contemporary artists.

Just past Absarokee, you can detour 4 miles off the beaten byway on Nye Road to the pleasant cottonwood oasis of **Fishtail** (pop. 78), an L-shaped wide spot that hugs two briskly moving forks of West Rosebud Creek. Stop first for homemade pizza or sandwiches at the cuter-than-cute, white-and-red **Fishtail General Store** (406-328-4441), a community gathering spot that has been "selling a little bit of everything since 1900"—making it the oldest continuously operating mercantile in Montana in its original location.

Attractive country barns are part of the bucolic landscape in the Stillwater Valley

These days the store has everything from soup to nuts and bolts. Made-in-Montana gifts, sundries, DVD rentals, and fishing and hunting gear make room for local honey, pistachios, made-to-order deli sandwiches, freshly crafted pizza, huge homemade cookies, sweet rolls, and divine cheesecakes. Owners Bill and Katy Martin bought the store as a retirement project and have been welcomed into the community. One visit and you'll soon see why. Up the road, beyond the village of **Dean**, is **Nye** (pop. 305), home to a buffalo jump, a three-room motel, a restaurant/casino, and the country's only palladium mine.

Returning to MT 78 either on the paved road or a scenic gravel road along the Stillwater River, the next stop over a small divide and just off the highway is **Roscoe** (pop. 106), another shade-tree oasis—this one along East Rosebud Creek. An early postmistress renamed the town after one of her horses. You can't drive anywhere south of I-90 without eventually seeing a bumper sticker asking "Where the hell is Roscoe Montana," a successful marketing campaign driven by the popular **Grizzly Bar** (406-328-6789). Along the way to Roscoe, look for two historical points: one marking the site of what had been the Crow Nation capital until the U.S. government reneged on a treaty, the other noting a challenging descent on the famed Bozeman Trail. Past Roscoe, MT 78 skips past little **Luther** and undulates toward the Beartooths, signaling your arrival in **Red Lodge** (pop. 2,400).

Save at least a day and perhaps two to explore the museums, galleries, and bountiful boutiques of this alluring foothills town, which is rapidly losing its distinction as the least-discovered gateway to Yellowstone. Once a raucous coal-mining center with more than 20 saloons and nearly as many ethnic neighborhoods, Red Lodge is decidedly tamer but still abuzz with energy. Possibly named for a breakaway band of Crow who erected a red teepee, the town is squeezed between grassy benches against the broad eastern shoulder of the Beartooths. Even when the Beartooth Highway is closed, Red Lodge remains a popular winter destination for its skiing and snowmobiling. The town also stages numerous unique events (www.redlodge.com/calendar) during its shoulder seasons to bolster a year-round economy.

Wandering the attractive main drag on foot can take hours, but leave time to spin off the beaten byway onto MT 308 and drive over a small divide to **Smith Mine No. 3.** You can park and walk amid the remnants of the worst coal-mine disaster in Montana history (71 perished). Another 7 arid miles east on MT 308 is **Bearcreek** (pop. 83) and a less somber attraction: the famed Bear Creek Downs pig races at **Bear Creek Saloon & Steak-**

house (406-446-3481). Yes, pig races. These little piggies go wee-wee-wee all the way around a dirt track, cheered on by bettors, every Thursday through Sunday in the summer. The unconventional entertainment began in 1988 as a way to spark business after the infamous fires that burned one-third of Yellowstone took a bite out of tourism. Along the way back to Red Lodge, the **Washoe Quilt Shoppe** (406-446-4094) is the lone business in **Washoe** (pop. 21) but has brisk traffic in part because quilting is such a passion in Montana's rural counties.

Back in Red Lodge, you may want to grab some essential snacks for the journey to the pass. Stock up from a staggering array of candy—including many hard-to-find varieties—at the **Montana Candy Emporium** (406-446-1119), open every day except Christmas. You can also sit a spell, sample local brews at the transformed **Red Lodge Ale Brewing Company** (406-

Everything from soup to nuts—pistachios are locally sourced—are in stock at the Fishtail General Store.

The future for Absarokee's Big Yellow House, which is known for its carpets and felted items from Kyrgyzstan, was uncertain in early 2011.

446-0243), and wait for a panini or baked sandwich for the road. Once literally a hole in the wall of the brewery, the taproom has an updated, yuppified look, but draws the same outstanding drafts.

Shortly after leaving Red Lodge, US 212 enters a broad U-shaped valley and begins zigging and zagging up the face of a pine-studded granite mountain. Be prepared with a jacket or fleece because the temperatures can drop as much as 30 degrees in the next 20 miles. Up, up, and up—the road seems to rise forever. Pines and firs give way to the prehistoric whitebark pine, which is making a last stand in these mountains. Enjoy the trees while you can. Armies of pine bark beetles, a warming climate enabling them to survive once-brutal winters, are killing conifers by the millions in all but the highest elevations—most notably the Beartooth. Prolific snows linger into July here and create a unique opportunity for skiers who want to avoid buying a lift ticket at **Red Lodge Mountain** (406-255-6973). Many schuss through the trees to lower portions of the highway, where they hitch a lift back to their car—or even higher—for more runs.

Just before the East Summit is the impressive **Rock Creek Vista Site**, with its sweeping views of the canyon far below. The highway has now reached the alpine tundra, nearly a mile higher in elevation than Red Lodge. Early visitors are usually treated to a blaze of such wildflowers as columbine and Indian paintbrush, which emerge after the long, harsh winter to make a colorful splash during their brief bloom window. A string of alpine lakes shimmers in the sunlight. Pull off the road and hike one of the dozens of Forest Service trails toward glacial lakes and other spectacular scenery in the Absaroka-Beartooth Wilderness. The area looks much the way it did when General Phillip Sheridan made the first documented crossing of the plateau on horseback in 1882. The 14-mile roundtrip **Black Canyon Lake** hike captures the essence of the mighty Beartooths and can be completed in one day. Crossing the Montana-Wyoming border, a favorite shorter hike is the **Beartooth Loop,** a National Recreation Trail that includes the oft-photographed Gardner Lake. At the East Summit, a chairlift seems to disappear into the invisible. This is the **Twin Lakes Headwall**, and skiing camps are conducted here in June and July, after snowmelt allows access but enough remains on the shaded north face to allow topflight training opportunities for Olympic hopefuls.

After traversing the tundra on the plateau for several miles and beginning a lengthy descent below the West Summit, you'll eventually arrive at the no-place-like-it **Top of the World Store** (307-587-5368). You have now crossed into Wyoming and are a little past the midway point to Cooke City. At 9,400 feet in elevation, you'll find intermittent phone service—they ask that you not call for weather conditions—and limited electricity, but a world of warmth from the folks who welcome you into their high-elevation harbor. The store was built along Beartooth Lake while the highway was under construction in 1934 then moved to its current site in 1964. If you want to wet a line in a Wyoming lake or stream, Cowboy State licenses are sold here—along with gas, snacks, maps, souvenirs, and just about anything else an outdoor person needs. Rentals for a wide variety of outdoor activities are also available.

From the Top of the World, the Beartooth Highway's complexion changes but remains attractive. One of the most photographed sites on

the way down to Cooke City is the **Index Overlook**. It provides an unob-
structed view into the North Absaroka Wilderness and of the pointy
11,708-foot Pilot Peak and its sister mountain, 10,709-foot Index Peak,
both carved by glaciers. A short distance later is **Clay Butte Lookout**, one of
the few fire lookouts easily accessible from a paved highway. It's a 2-mile
drive or hike to the lookout, which has marvelous panoramic views and
interpretive information about the scars of the 1988 fires that nearly left
Cooke City in ashes. After the junction of WY 296, the road follows the
meandering Clarks Fork of the Yellowstone River, an angler's paradise.
The highway soon crosses back into Montana and descends gently through
towering pine and spruce into **Cooke City** (pop. 140), the end of the road
coming from the other direction in winter. Like Red Lodge, Cooke City
has its genesis as a mining town; unlike Red Lodge, its economy is narrow—Yellowstone visitors in summer, snowmobilers and wolf watchers in
winter. The lodging and dining befits such uniformity. The **Cooke City
Store** (406-838-2234), built in 1886, still has some of its original hardware
and is worth a stop for ice cream, souvenirs, and a brief peek at history.
For more charm but fewer lodging and dining opportunities, continue
along Soda Butte Creek toward the park's northeast entrance another 3
miles to **Silver Gate** (pop. 15), where year-round non-motorized peace is
the antithesis of its motor-happy neighbor. On the way, look for the incon-
spicuous sign on the right for **Hartman Gallery** (406-838-2296), an exten-
sion of Dan and Cindy Hartman's house in a conifer thicket. You can view
or purchase paintings of stunning landscapes and/or wildlife—and may
catch a glimpse of a resident pine marten, if you're lucky.

Silver Gate has its roots in mining and has an equally breathtaking
Absaroka backdrop, but the similarities stop there. The entire population,
a dozen or so year-rounders, has made a conscientious effort to be the quiet
alternative to neighboring Cooke City, with emphasis on sustainable,
human-powered recreation. Also, here is the stately and reputedly haunted **Range Riders Lodge**, once one of the two or three largest freestanding
log structures in the nation. The former bordello rooms upstairs are available for large group bookings, and the lodge frequently hosts musical
events and other activities during the high season. For your hiking, skiing,
and climbing needs, the **Silvertip Mountain Center** (800-863-0807) gears
its retail and rental inventory to the season. Amiable Jay and his partner
Laurie, both accomplished outdoor adventurers, can also give tips and
takes on the area. New business on the scene in late 2010 was **Stop the Car**

And they're off! Pigs trot their way around the track behind Bear Creek Saloon.

Trading Post (406-838-2130), the year-round place to stock up on convenience items and made-in-Montana gifts.

Silver Gate and Cooke City are in some of the best grizzly bear habitat in America. Locals have grown accustomed to living with bears in their midst, but even they were shook up in July 2010 when an undernourished sow with three cubs attacked and killed a sleeping fisherman at Soda Butte Campground. It was the first bear-related fatality in Greater Yellowstone in a quarter century. Whenever in grizzly country, it's mandatory to bring bear spray, make noise, store food properly, and travel in parties of at least four if possible.

From Silver Gate, it's a mere 1 mile to the park. You can continue your journey by taking the only year-round road in Yellowstone through the Lamar Valley. But that's another trip described in *Great Destinations: Yellowstone and Grand Teton National Parks and Jackson Hole* from Countryman Press.

Best Places to Bunk

Absarokee: For the more economy-minded, **Stillwater Lodge** ($/$$, 406-328-4899) has six cute and tightly quartered rooms on the main drag across from the Whitebird Gallery.

Fishtail: The **Fiddler Creek Cabins** ($$, 406-328-4949) are three well-equipped and comfortable cabins in the country with decks featuring views of the Beartooth Mountains.

Red Lodge: The signature place to stay is the historic, redbrick **Pollard Hotel** ($$/$$$, 406-446-0001) in the heart of downtown. The Pollard has accommodated the likes of Buffalo Bill, Jeremiah "Liver-Eating" Johnston, and Martha Jane Cannary-Burke, aka Calamity Jane, among other frontier celebrities. The building fell into disrepair, then was renovated and reopened in 1994 as a fully modern hotel and dining room that retains much of its former charm. For upscale-plus B&B lodging, the **Rocky Fork Inn** ($$$, 406-446-2967) has six suites in a sprawling log structure overlooking Rock Creek. **Gallagher's Irish Rose B&B** ($$, 406-446-0303), closed April/May and October/November, is a century-old home with original artwork from Leah Gallagher; it has three themed rooms reflecting the town's Irish roots. The **Beartooth Hideaway Inn & Cabins** ($/$$, 406-446-2488), formerly a Super 8, has a swimming pool and is probably the most appealing of the motor-inn-style lodging, though the newly renovated **Yodeler** ($/$$, 406-446-1435) is comfortable and won't disappoint. To feel as if you're in Sun Valley or Aspen, the stylish **Rock Creek Resort** ($$$/$$$$, 406-446-1111), 5 miles south of Red Lodge at the mouth of the mountains, is spectacular yet invitingly understated. Townhouses, condos, and standard rooms come in a variety of decors ranging from Guatemalan to Montanan, and you'll be surprised to learn that rooms start at an anti-Aspen $125. The out-of-the-ordinary **Top of the World Motel** ($, 307-587-5368) is open year-round and is actually more charming than Cooke City's bunking options; however, it's often booked for construction workers so reservations are highly recommended.

Silver Gate: A personal favorite is the attractive **Pine Edge Cabins** ($$/$$$, 406-838-2371), the only year-round lodging in this one-block village. The remodeled units are part of a collection that includes the **Silver Gate** and **Whispering Pines** cabins, which are open during the summer season. The view from the Pine Edge Cabins is of towering Mount Republic, and during winter months, guests often see silver fox, moose, and a lone bison affectionately named Jackson.

Alternative Bunking

Absarokee: Paintbrush Adventures ($$$$, 406-328-4158) has a cushy cabin on the Stillwater River—you can literally fish right off your deck—that sleeps eight for $225 per night, with weekly and monthly discounts negotiable. Dividing the rate among eight makes this a steal. Located on the Barron Ranch, the home and apartment above the garage are part of Montana Bunkhouses Working Ranch Vacations, a group that is trying to bolster local economies by offering authentic Montana experiences.

Belfry: Another Montana Bunkhouses offering is the **Beartooth River Ranch** ($$$$, 406-664-3181), just over the hill from Red Lodge. The lodge is located on the Clark's Fork of the Yellowstone River.

Fishtail: The cozy **Swallow's Nest** ($$, 406-328-4236) cabin was converted from a small shack between horse pastures in a rural-residential area. It doesn't look like much on the outside, but its well-crafted interior makes for pleasant cocooning. The cabin accommodates two, has a full kitchen, and is available by the night, week, or month.

Silver Gate: Laurie Hinck, a full-time resident who grew up in the area, has two traditional log cabins for rent at the **Log Cabin B&B** ($$, 800-863-0807), each with two double beds. The showers are a short walk away. The best part of the $99 a night rate is the full breakfast at the Log Cabin Inn.

Camping: Campers and picnickers might like the shade of the towering cottonwoods drinking from the Yellowstone River at the **Itch-Kep-Pe Park**. The Custer National Forest in Montana and Shoshone National Forest in Wyoming have numerous campgrounds along the route, 14 with a total of 226 campsites within close proximity to the highway. There are six on the Montana side before US 212 begins its precipitous switchback rise out of Rock Creek Canyon, two on the plateau, one each at Island and Beartooth lakes, three along the Clarks Fork of the Yellowstone, and three just outside Cooke City. Expect chilly nights—the higher the elevation, the chillier. In Fishtail, another appealing choice is camping with quick and easy fishing access at Rosebud Isle situated along the banks of the West Rosebud Creek.

Best Eats

Columbus: At the top of the list is the **307 Bar, Grill & Casino** ($$, 406-322-4511, B/L/D). Once dubbed "The Bloody Bucket" for its frequent brawls, it's now a family-friendly joint where wine and beer drinkers sit side by side. It serves good-enough-to-brake-for burgers, melt-in-your-mouth pot roast, and a distinctive variety of entrées in a log-furniture, art-on-the-walls setting. Understated **Whitlock's Stillwater Steakhouse** ($$, 406-322-8677, B/L/D) is a meat, potatoes, and fried food (alligator tail) kinda place that serves up everything from rib eye to walleye.

Absarokee: The **Rosebud Cafe** ($, 406-328-6969, B/L/D) has rancher-sized portions of chicken-fried steak, Mexican cuisine, and hearty breakfasts of steak and eggs or piles of buttermilk pancakes; you can also get a sack lunch to go.

Fishtail: Wrap your hands around a half-pound burger, halibut sandwich, or any number of appealing dinner choices at the **Cowboy Bar & Supper Club** ($$, 406-328-4288, L/D). The starters aren't the usual: deep-fried green beans, spinach artichoke wonton, and crab cakes. Have dinner in the bar or in the cheerful country-Italian dining room.

Come as you are, grizzled or not, for a dinner and libations at the Grizzly Bar in Roscoe. John Baker

Dean: Ten miles up Nye Road across from Fishtail Butte is **Montana Jack's Bar & Grill** ($$, 406-328-4110, L/D/Brunch), which has reinvented itself a few times; previously it was Montana Hanna's. Jack's bar and dining setup has a floor-to-ceiling rock fireplace separating two eating areas. The ambitious menu focuses on smoked barbecue meats (chicken, pork, ribs) and mixes up cowboy traditional with southern cookin'. An example of Montana Jack's creative efforts at luring people into the hinterlands: an exquisite dinner paired with wine from Sineann, a small winery in Oregon. In fact, the wine and beer list, one of the state's best, is predominantly Pacific Northwest.

Roscoe: The **Grizzly Bar** ($$, 406-328-6789, L/D) is one of Montana's most iconic steakhouses, thanks to its hefty prime rib, king-sized burgers, large patio seating area, and ubiquitous bumper stickers.

Red Lodge: Plan your drive so that you can dine in Red Lodge more than once, for there are many outstanding choices. **The Pollard Hotel** ($$, 406-446-0001, B/D) has a menu that changes seasonally, an extensive wine list, and a full bar. **Bridge Creek Backcountry Kitchen & Wine Bar** ($, 406-446-9900, L/D) best represents the new Red Lodge with its emphasis on fresh, nouveau, and local—except for its extraordinary international wine selection. This is also where a clam chowder aficionado can test Bridge Creek's "famous for thirteen years" version. Representing the old Red Lodge is the **Carbon County Steakhouse** ($$/$$$, 406-446-4025, L/D, Wed.–Sun.), which has "cowboy cuisine" with hormone-free beef, bison, and elk, as well as"not from the ranch" seafood, and fresh mussels flown in from the Pacific Northwest on Wednesdays and Fridays. More casual and suited for a late lunch/early dinner or chips-salsa-margarita break is **Bogart's** ($$, 406-446-1784, L/D), an always-crowded Mexican and pizza watering hole with a rustic western feel accentuated by its brawny back bar. The **Cafe Regis** ($, 406-446-1941, B/L), once an other-era grocery store, is owned by a vegetarian who knows how to take care of fellow greenies and health-food fans. To see where the regulars hang out for coffee and conversation, try the historic **City Bakery** ($, 406-446-2100, B/L), known for something called *schnecken*—a rich concoction of cinnamon, butter, cream cheese, and nuts in a roll; it'll have you yearning for more. City Bakery became famous for its après ski loaf of French bread and slab of butter, but if we had to choose a favorite, a maple bar or old-fashioned dunking doughnut with a simple cup of coffee would win. Breakfast or lunch at the **Red Lodge Café** ($$, 406-446-1619, B/L/D), with its almost life-sized murals, log furniture, and neon teepee sign, is more about tradition and history than memorable food. But at printing time, the café had new owners and things could change.

Cool off with a cone full of soft ice cream or enjoy a burger creekside at

Red Lodge's oldest drive-in, the **Red Box Car Drive-In** ($, 406-446-2152, L/D), housed in a 100-year-old—you guessed it—boxcar.

Bearcreek: The **Bear Creek Saloon & Steakhouse** ($$, 406-446-3481, D, Thur.–Sun.) is best known for the pig races out back, but the flatiron steaks are drive-worthy; the restaurant is open May through September and December through March. Just a note: You can't eat at the bar, so call ahead or be prepared to wait for a table. For a more economical and equally memorable meal, go next door to the **Hungry Bear Bakery** ($$, 406-446-9177, B/L/D). Kathy Arnold's secret-recipe hamburgers, banana-cream pie, and rich homemade chocolate layer cake are the draw here; closing time is 6:30 PM during the summer and 5:30 PM in the off-season, but if you're late or linger, you won't be turned away or shoved out the door.

Cooke City: The year-round **Miner's Saloon** ($/$$, 406-838-2214, L/D) is as much museum as it is a tavern, with most of its mining and outdoor recreation artifacts on the ceiling. Upscale dinner specials are a welcome sight, but Miner's is best known for its large pizzas and burger with fries plate. The seasonal **Beartooth Café** ($$, 406-838-2475, B/L/D) is the place to sit on a breezy deck and listen to live music or hear the latest on grizzly bear sightings while sipping on one of 130 beer choices and digging into a hand-cut sirloin steak. For a seemingly out of place change of pace, you'll find gourmet fare at **The Bistro** ($$/$$$, 406-838-2160, B/L/D), which warms the hearts of winter visitors by reopening in late December (post-Christmas) after a short autumn hiatus.

Silver Gate: Currently the only restaurant in town, **Log Cabin Café and B&B** ($$, 800-863-0807, B/L/D, May–Sept.), is favored for its lightly breaded and grilled Idaho trout, which you can get with eggs for breakfast or as an entrée for lunch or dinner. Another signature item is their flown-in Alaskan sockeye, which is either prepared lightly smoked or as a simple filet. They're also rightfully proud of their burgers, made from grass-fed beef from Belfry. Save room for spoon-licking pumpkin-bread pudding.

Best Bars

Bearcreek: Grab a cold one, place your bet at the window, and get ready to cheer on your porker at the **Bear Creek Saloon's** (406-446-3481) summer pig races. Folks come from as far away as Billings and Cody to help with a good cause: Proceeds help pay college tuition for a deserving Carbon County student. Although you can't eat at the bar, you can whet your appetite with $2.50 bottled beer or equally cheap, generously poured, well drinks served in a plastic cup to take out to the track's viewing deck. Oh, and the food—emphasis on steaks—is pretty good too. No pork served, of course.

Fishtail: Like the General Store, the well-worn but well-kept and laid-back **Cowboy Bar & Supper Club** (406-328-4288) is a longtime icon for shooting the bull and imbibing. While enjoying a cold beer or cocktail, savor a cut-to-order steak, chicken, or—and this might seem redundant in Montana—a mighty impressive burger. During the rowdy annual Testy Festy, you can have the rare privilege of sampling beer-battered calf testicles—locally produced, naturally.

Dean: Although technically off the beaten byway, it's worth the extra 10-mile drive to the classy **Montana Jack's Bar & Grill** where the menu ranges from chuck-wagon-style BBQ to pasta dishes to entrée salads. Live entertainment and a an outstanding regional wine list are beyond what you would expect this far from any main drag.

The Perfect Weekend

Start your Friday at the **Museum of the Beartooths** in Columbus and then mosey into Absarokee to appreciate the work of Montana artists at the **Whitebird Gallery**. Reach Fishtail in the late morning and wander into the **Fishtail General Store** to pick up a platter-sized cookie or sweet roll for the trip. Arrive in Roscoe in time for lunch at the **Grizzly Bar**, then meander toward the Beartooth Mountains and Red Lodge in time to check into the **Pollard Hotel** for the night. Once you've settled and had appetizers and a beverage in the restaurant, jump back in your car and drive over the hill toward Bearcreek. Pause for a moment at **Smith Mine No. 3** to remember the 71 fallen miners. Continue on a short distance to the **Bear Creek Saloon & Steakhouse** for a Montana-sized steak and a memorable evening watching the pigs run in the summer. Take a break between bets for homemade chocolate layer cake or banana-cream pie next door at the **Hungry Bear Bakery**. Return to the Pollard for the night.

In the morning, get a bag of sweet treats and a *schnecken* at the historic **City Bakery**. Wander the shops, galleries, and boutiques of downtown Red Lodge before a healthy lunch at the **Cafe Regis**. For an ultrasweet

BEARTOOTH HIGHWAY SOFTENED DEPRESSION IN RED LODGE

At the turn of the previous century, Yellowstone National Park was becoming an international tourist destination. Such gateway communities as West Yellowstone, Gardiner, and Cody were riding a tidal wave of economic success since automobiles were legally allowed into the park for the first time in 1915. Though separated from Yellowstone by some of the region's most rugged terrain, Red Lodge nevertheless wanted a piece of the action—especially after the nearby coal mine closed in 1924.

A road over the rocky Beartooth Plateau, city fathers surmised, would give tourists direct access to the park's northeast entrance and enable businesses in Cooke City to tap a mother lode of gold in the New World Mining District about 3 miles from Yellowstone's boundary. They weren't the first to consider travel over the Beartooth—Indians had been doing it for thousands of years—but the task was daunting nonetheless. The grandiose vision was to punch a road into Rock Creek Canyon, carve switchbacks out of the side of a 4,000-foot mountain, lay pavement across the plateau's fragile tundra and 3-billion-year-old rocks, and then etch a serpentine route down the backside in Wyoming to Cooke City. It took years of planning.

But in 1931, as the darkness of the Great Depression enveloped a nation, construction began. Remarkably, it would take only five years, opening to great fanfare in 1936. Answering a letter in the 1970s from a fan inquiring about the most beautiful drives in America, CBS newsman Charles Kuralt, renowned for his regular "On the Road" features, responded "US 212."

Not surprisingly, keeping the Beartooth All-American Highway open and maintained is a chore. Wicked weather wreaks havoc on the road, requiring renovations that'll require patience from drivers in the coming years. In 2005, a mudslide ruined 13 sections of road and kept it closed all summer.

The road officially opens Memorial Day and closes Labor Day, though it's often possible to drive the route into October. Don't be surprised if you run into patches of snow—terrific summer photo-ops—at any time of year.

dessert, browse the aisles of the **Montana Candy Emporium** and stock up on some of the most varied candies found anywhere before beginning your ascent to the Beartooth Plateau. On the way up, pull over at **Rock Creek Vista** to take the short walk to a stunning viewpoint. Back on the road, check out the **Top of the World Store** and perhaps grab a hot coffee to mute the chill. On the way down toward Cooke City, pull over at the **Clarks**

Fork of the Yellowstone and Index Peak viewpoints. Finish the day with a salmon dinner at the Log Cabin Cafe in Silver Gate and a night (or two) in the Pine Edge Cabins (reservations highly recommended).

DETOUR: ONE FOR THE ROAD

The Paradise Valley
Livingston to Gardiner

Estimated length: 60 miles

Highlights: Yellowstone River, Chico Hot Springs, Pine Creek Tavern, Yellowstone National Park.

Getting there: Take Exit 333 off I-90 in Livingston.

In many ways, the visually appealing drive along the **Yellowstone River** embodies the new Montana. Lured by the jagged peaks of the Absarokas, trout-rich waters of the Yellowstone, and proximity to the world's first national park, both the well-heeled and off-the-grid sorts call the aptly named Paradise Valley home. In the beginning, the name came from the Crow, who once thrived on the prolific wildlife drawn here in winter when ferocious winds scoured the grasslands of snow. The Crow, aka Absaroka ("children of the large beaked bird"), are gone, but the name and the unparalleled beauty remain.

Livingston, immortalized in song by Jimmy Buffett with "Livingston Saturday Night," "Monday Monday," and, reputedly, "Cheeseburger in Paradise," is an old railroad town that has become an artists colony with more professional writers per capita than any town in the United States. Stock up on wine, cheese, and specialty foods at the Gourmet Cellar. From Livingston, drive south on US 89 through a gap in the mountains. When the valley opens, look for a left turn on East River Road and cross the Yellowstone River.

Drive along the river and absorb the views of the Absarokas. For a down-home weekend evening in the summer, dance under the pines and stars to live music at the **Pine Creek Tavern**. Or take a break for a soak and five-star dinner at **Chico Hot Springs**, 30 miles south of Livingston. The walls of the historic main lodge are adorned with photos of one of the springs' biggest fans, the actor Warren Beatty. At **Pray**, cross over the river to US 89 and the homespun **Emigrant Bakery** to grab some baked goods and soup before returning to East River Road.

East River Road eventually returns to US 89, and just after the turnoff for Tom Miner Basin, the highway squeezes through Yankee Jim Canyon. At the southern end of Yankee Jim, look to the right for a unique rock formation called **Devil's Slide**.

Gardiner is a raw town that retains much of its frontier character and is home to many Yellowstone National Park employees. For eats, the **K Bar & Cafe** has average ambience but a surprisingly excellent pizza. The **Tumbleweed Bookstore & Café** is the place for a veggie sandwich, earthy soup, coffee or tea, and Internet access. **Helen's Corral Drive-In** (summers) was famed regionally for her "hateful hamburger" until she passed away, leaving the popular drive-in for sale and with an uncertain future in 2011. New to the scene is the **Cowboy Lodge & Grille** where you can satisfy your hunger with southern-style BBQ in pork, chicken, brisket, or ribs and then settle in for the night in one of the thoughtfully redecorated townhouse-style rooms. **Rosie's Cafe** is the latest seasonal restaurant trying to provide some semblance of upscale dining, though the seasonal dining room at **Mammoth Hot Springs**, 5 miles up the hill in the park, has a creative menu. Before entering the park, stop at the classy **Yellowstone Association** headquarters near the Roosevelt Arch; the educational and interpretive group refurbished the 1903 Reamer Building and has Yellowstone-related displays, books, gifts, and helpful tips for sightseeing in the park.

The end of this route is at the park entrance. The arch, an impressive stone-basalt structure, was built in 1903—31 years after the creation of the park—to commemorate the arrival of the railroad to Gardiner, bringing tourists to Yellowstone's doorstep. The first stone was laid by President Theodore Roosevelt, a former mason. Look for bison, elk, and pronghorn grazing or resting in the grassy meadows at the park's edge.

Shiras moose are frequently seen foraging on willows along the Red Rock River.

Solitude at Altitude: The Centennial Valley

West Yellowstone to Monida

Estimated length: 74 miles
Estimated time: 3 to 5 hours

Highlights: Wildlife viewing, exceptional birding, hiking, Red Rock Pass, Fountain of the Missouri, Red Rock Lakes National Wildlife Refuge, Elk Lake Resort, Lakeview.

Getting there: From I-90, there are several ways to reach the Centennial Valley—all of them scenic. Coming from Butte on I-15, make any necessary stops for gas, food, or lodging in Dillon, Lima, or Dell before leaving the freeway at Monida, the last exit before Idaho and little more than a dilapidated collection of empty buildings. Drive through the remnants of this former railroad town and follow the signs for Lakeview and the Red Rock Lakes National Wildlife Refuge, both 28 gravel miles ahead. This is the west end of the valley and the road less traveled.

To begin at the east end, take US 191 from Bozeman through the scenic Gallatin Canyon and northwest corner of Yellowstone National Park to the community of West Yellowstone. Continue west on US 20 over the Continental Divide into Idaho. At the junction of US 20 and ID 87, turn right and drive along the north shore of Henrys Lake. Turn left on FS 055 around the west end of the lake, then veer right on Red Rock Pass Road. In West Yellowstone, stock up on any necessary goodies and fuel up because

Three pioneer cemeteries are within close proximity to the main road through the Centennial Valley.

you won't see a single backcountry store until you reach I-15.

If you're coming down US 287 from Three Forks, you can shave a few miles by turning right on MT 87 over the Madison River and heading over Raynolds Pass into Idaho, where the road becomes ID 87. You'll quickly see Henrys Lake; turn right on FS 055. The entire Centennial Valley route is on gravel and dirt, and the shaded east side of Red Rock Pass can get especially soupy after spring runoff or a hard rainstorm. A high-clearance and/or four-wheel-drive vehicle is recommended, though unnecessary when conditions are dry.

Overview

Ask most Montana residents with an appreciation for wild country where they go to see and feel the mystical open-range of 150 years ago, and chances are good they'll take a reverent breath and utter "the Centennial Valley." It's so remote, even for Montana, that you must leave the state to get there from the east end. Upon the second of two ascents to the Continental Divide, including a brief foray past log vacation homes on Idaho's Henrys Lake, visitors quickly realize why Montanans have the same regard for this place as they do their horses.

The Centennial is a broad, largely unscarred plain with lakes, marshes, sagebrush, a handful of sprawling cattle ranches, one tiny unincorporated community (Lakeview, no services), and the Red Rock River meandering through its heart. It's surrounded by the burly shoulders of the Centennial Mountains to the south and the tips of the rugged Snowcrests, Blacktails, and Gravellys to the north. It's a place where winged creatures outnumber bipeds by about 10,000 to one. Depending on your mindset, an aura of serenity or loneliness exists here, and there is a palpable separation from the modern world. Also making the Centennial extraordinary: The 385,000-acre valley and mountain range run east–west, an oddity in the Northern Rockies. It's thus a critical wildlife migration corridor between Greater Yellowstone—which is essentially an ecological island in a sea of development—and the wilds of central Idaho. Birders will be in avian heaven in the 44,963-acre Red Rock Lakes National Wildlife Refuge, which features more than 240 species. The refuge was created in 1935 because of its importance as a stopover for such migratory waterfowl as the endangered trumpeter swan and prehistoric-sounding sandhill crane. Almost all the native wildlife from 200 years ago still roams the valley—the notable exception being bison, which would seem right at home on the grasslands.

It's difficult to imagine, especially if you enter from the east side, that the Centennial was once a relatively heavily traveled valley. Before E. H. Harriman of the Union Pacific Railroad punched his Oregon Short Line through the mountains from Ashton, Idaho, to West Yellowstone in 1908, one of the primary routes to Yellowstone National Park was through the Centennial. Railroad passengers disembarked at Monida and took the Centennial Stage to West Yellowstone, exchanging horses every 15 miles. Former president

Teddy Roosevelt, perhaps the father of American conservation, reputedly took the journey once. Lakeview was once a base for railroad workers who commuted to where the main Northern Pacific line crosses Monida Pass—which draws its name from the first three letters of both states.

The Centennial Valley—named by early cattle rancher Rachael Orr, who first saw the valley during America's centennial in 1876—has been preserved for many reasons, not the least of which is remoteness. The valley has been spared mineral exploration and rapacious logging. And somewhere along the way, the 15 multigenerational ranch families that own 90 percent of the 100,000 acres of private land in the Centennial have cultivated a conservation ethic. The ranchers, federal Bureau of Land Management, and The Nature Conservancy—which owns much of the remaining 10 percent of private land—have forged a partnership with a mission dedicated to preserving the Centennial's wide-open spaces and sense of history. Their shared vision has fostered a balance between utilitarian use of the land and preserving wildlife habitat so future generations can drive the bumpy 51 miles and see some of our most iconic critters. Included are endangered grizzly bears, wolves, Shiras moose, bighorn sheep, eagles, and trumpeter swans.

Hitting the Road

To fully appreciate the lack of intrusion into this wonderland, start your journey at **West Yellowstone** (pop. 1,511), a crowded metropolis compared to the rest of the route. Once a getaway for Las Vegas hoteliers and a few of their sordid friends—hence the Desert Inn Motel, for example—this outpost enveloped by lodgepole pines is trying to evolve from a rubber-tomahawk souvenir-shop image to one of more sophistication. For nearly five decades, its winter existence has revolved around snowmobiling, and its summer season has been marked by families in station wagons and minivans, both groups eager to see Old Faithful. If you're looking for activities other than what the natural world has to offer, the **IMAX Theater** (406-646-4100) and **Grizzly & Wolf Discovery Center** (406-646-7001/800-257-2570), adjacent to each other near the edge of town, will fill the bill. If you miss seeing some of the wildlife in the park, catch them in living color—literally—at the Discovery Center where the bears don't hibernate because they have a year-round source of food. West Yellowstone has plenty of lodging and dining during the summer, but many businesses close during the winter and shoulder seasons.

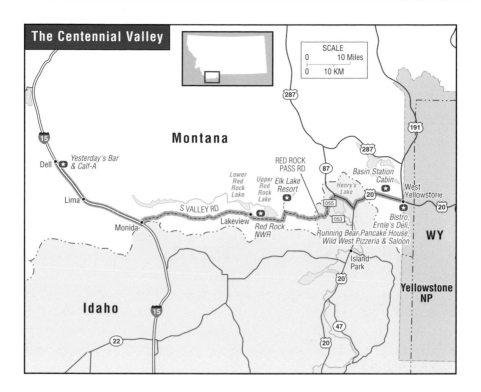

As you head west out of West Yellowstone, look closely at the mountain range in full view straight ahead. With a little imagination, it's easy to see why the 10,080-foot peak along the Continental Divide is called Lionhead Mountain. You'll soon be over the pass into Idaho. Though this is a book about Montana, we suggest spending a day on **Henrys Lake** trolling for legendary trophy trout. The sweeping valley before you is the key wildlife connector between Yellowstone and the Centennial. To the southwest, you'll see what looks like a giant golf ball on top of a mountain. This is a radio tower atop Sawtelle Mountain, the eastern terminus of the Centennials. If you turn right on ID 87, you'll meet up with FS 055 in about 6 miles.

If you continue south on US 20 toward **Island Park, Idaho**, you'll turn right on FS 053 in 6 miles. Either way, the two gravel Forest Service roads meet just off the southwest corner of Henrys Lake, about 3.5 miles shy of **Red Rock Pass**. After passing a few modest log homes, the road ascends through aspens to the pass—and a step back in time.

Red Rock Pass is more of a long bump in the road. After a brief descent through fir and pine, the Centennial's wide world of wonder begins to unfurl, with an endless horizon between five mountain ranges. There are

Commonly seen in the sagebrush, pronghorn are the fastest land mammal in North America.

no homes and few power lines to mar the view—only a few fence lines and occasional mailbox. Immediately to the south are the towering Centennials. Tucked deep into the forest, Brower Spring, aka the **Fountain of the Missouri,** trickles from the flanks of Mount Jefferson at 9,030 feet in elevation and begins a 2,530-mile journey to its meeting with the Mississippi at St. Louis. No waters anywhere in the United States travel farther. It's a strenuous hike into wild country, but if you're fit and determined, you'll be one of few Americans to say they have sipped from the uppermost Missouri headwaters, which are marked by a pile of rocks; an easier trail comes from Sawtelle Mountain. Park at the Hell Roaring Creek Trailhead and give yourself a good half day to cover the territory, and bring bear spray. If you're not comfortable going on your own, **Hellroaring Adventures** (406-57-4025) and **Centennial Outfitters** (406-276-3463) offer backcountry pack trips, the former to a yurt in the winter and the latter to cabins in the summer.

Back on Red Rock Pass Road, you'll follow the south shore of Upper Red Rock Lake. Look for trumpeter swans and ducks on the lake, sandhill cranes and white-faced ibis in the grasses, and Shiras moose browse on the willows. On the other side of the road, look for pronghorn in the sage-brush and elk moving in and out of the tree line—maybe even a wolf or bear. If you brought your fly rod, these clean, cold waters offer great fishing, including the chance to catch (and release) the increasingly rare westslope cutthroat trout.

Welcome to the **Red Rock Lakes National Wildlife Refuge** (406-276-3536), literally the country's last best place for trumpeter swans. Some 30 to 50 can be seen at any given time (in pairs and family groups), up to 100 cygnets and mature birds in the summer. The northeast corner is federally protected wilderness, one of the few marshes in the country given a designation that strictly prohibits development, mechanized vehicles, and even chainsaws for cutting firewood. There are no established human trails; any noticeably trafficked route across the grasslands was created by wildlife. The refuge is also a National Natural Landmark.

Most of the human activity on the refuge begins at the headquarters in **Lakeview** (pop. 86). A drive-through kiosk provides maps and an overview, and a cabin houses U.S. Fish & Wildlife Service staff who happily offer more detailed insights and information. Though abundant bird life is everywhere, you'll be thankful for bringing a spotting scope. Access to both Upper and Lower Red Rock Lakes is limited. Hiking is allowed anywhere, but it can be dicey; wander off a game trail, and you could find yourself thigh deep in a bog. The best time to see the widest variety of wildlife here is in the fall, before snowdrifts close Red Rock Pass to autos.

Lakeview is mostly a collection of small cabins. Aside from the refuge, it's also the home of the **International Center for Earth Concerns,** a non-profit that preserves and protects habitat in the United States and as far away as Kenya. Headquarters are located in a renovated historic structure that's hard to miss. The center has also restored and preserved settler homes in the valley.

Heading west, you'll notice Lakeview's connection to the outside world: telephone poles stretching to the horizon. The valley broadens even more, and thousands of black dots appear amid the grass and sage. These are Angus cattle tended by ranching families that have braved long, fierce winters and isolation for more than a century. These sweeping views remain much the same for the next 28 miles, with only the mountains to the north changing—from the southern tip of the rugged Gravellys to the southern edge of the even more rugged Snowcrests. The more adventurous and free-way-averse might consider turning north on FS 202, an improved gravel road that slices between the Snowcrest and Blacktail ranges en route to a meeting with I-15 at Dillon. As of winter 2010, lands in the Gravellys, Snowcrests, and Blacktails were under consideration for the first wilderness designation in Montana in a quarter century—further ensuring that this remote country remains much the way it is well into the future.

If you continue on to I-15 at Monida, the first services are still another 15 miles to the northwest at Lima. For more conventional lodging and dining, continue to Dillon on I-15. Clark Canyon Reservoir is a well-used recreation site, and the Beaverhead River downstream from the dam is a favorite of trout fishermen, especially in the spring and early summer when other rivers are largely unfishable due to spring runoff. See the Big Hole Loop for more on Dillon.

Best Places to Bunk

West Yellowstone: Lodging is pretty homogenous in this theme-park-like town, ranging from clean and well-kept mom-and-pops to the standard chain motels. Six miles west of town on US 20 is the 200-acre **Bar N Ranch** ($$$$, 406-646-0300, May–Oct.), which has more upscale lodge rooms and cabins, with a made-to-order breakfast included. An added bonus: Guests have a section of the Madison River all to themselves for blue-ribbon trout fishing.

Centennial Valley: For the purist's Centennial Valley experience, stay at **Elk Lake Resort** ($$, 406-276-3282), a rustic and secluded getaway open seasonally and only accessible by snowmobile in the winter. The resort likes to say it's on the "backside of nowhere." The modest collection of seven cabins plus ranch house is still listed on many maps as Selby Resort, its former name. There's another lodging option in the valley: The **J Bar L** ($$$$, 406-684-5927), a working cattle ranch that raises grass-fed beef and offers an all-inclusive true western experience. Packages begin at three nights in a restored cabin near the ranch or in a renovated homestead on their acreage—helping out with the chores can be included, or not. The J Bar L is between the North Centennial Valley Road and the Red Rock River, downstream from Lower Red Rock Lake. To get to both Elk Lake Resort and the J Bar L, turn right on Elk Lake Road about 7 miles after ascending Red Rock Pass. Continue on Elk Lake Road about 4 miles to the resort, then turn left on North Side Road and go west about 8 miles to the ranch.

RED ROCKS TRUMPETS A CONSERVATION SUCCESS

More than a century ago, the large and elegant trumpeter swan was on the verge of extinction, its white plume coveted by easterners for their hats and quill pens. In the United States, the trumpeter—named for a call that sounds like a French horn—was making its last stand in Greater Yellowstone beginning in 1932. Many of the 69 remaining birds lived year-round in the wildlife refuge created to save them.

Today, Greater Yellowstone's trumpeter numbers are at about 380 year-round birds, including 45 nesting pairs. Add that to about 2,000 annual visitors from Canada, and you have a conservation success story nearly on a par with the bald eagle.

The magnificence of this bird starts with its size. Many trumpeters reach a height of 4 feet and stand up to 6 feet tall when craning their necks, giving it the distinction of being the largest waterfowl in North America. With their snow-white plumes, the trumpeter also is a standout on the landscape—even in winter, when they sequester themselves on unfrozen waterways.

The trumpeter's place isn't entirely secure, even in Greater Yellowstone. It's shy and extremely sensitive to changing conditions, such as encroachment from homes, agriculture, and recreational vehicles. Thus, The Trumpeter Swan Society is in the midst of an effort to increase numbers to about 540 swans and nearly triple nesting pairs in Greater Yellowstone.

Trumpeters are best viewed around Upper and Lower Red Rock Lakes. If you see a swan in the Centennial Valley between April and October, it's almost certainly a resident trumpeter because the migrants are back in Canada and tundra swans are scarce. If you can't get into the Centennial to see trumpeters in winter, an excellent spot is just south of Henrys Lake on the spring-fed Henry's Fork of the Snake River in Island Park, Idaho.

Lima: The **Mountain View Motel & RV Park** ($, 406-276-3535) just off the I-15 exit has clean, serviceable lodging for "bucks and does" as well as a made-in-Montana gift shop. **Jan's Café** ($, 406-276-3484) has two gussied-up cabins next to the diner that sleep up to six in each.

Dell: Just off the interstate is the **Stockyard Inn B&B** ($$, 406-276-3501), with seasonal lodging in six upscale western-themed rooms and a honeymoon suite with a Jacuzzi tub; it's open from summer through the autumn hunting seasons.

Alternative Bunking

Camping: In the Red Rock Lakes National Wildlife Refuge, the **Upper and Lower Red Rock Lake Campgrounds** are open year-round. They are accessible in winter only by snow machine and seldom filled—perfect for solitude and wildlife viewing. A bit primitive, you'll find Porta-Potties, potable water in the spring, fire rings (no chainsaws permitted), and picnic tables.

Forest Service Cabins/Lookouts: (Reservations: 877-444-6777 or www.recreation.gov.) The **Basin Station Cabin** (406-823-6961, $30/sleeps four) on the Gallatin National Forest is 2 miles off US 20 and along Denny Creek Road about 7 miles west of West Yellowstone, so it isn't the primitive experience one thinks of in terms of cabins and lookouts, but its accessibility is a bonus. For a serious sense of solitude, try the primitive **West Fork Cabin** (406-682-4253, $35/three, July–Mar.) on the West Fork of the Madison River on the Beaverhead-Deerlodge National Forest. As the crow flies, it's less than 10 miles due north of the North Side Road just east of Eureka Basin, but get a map from the Madison Ranger District when making reservations. Another great primitive experience is the **Antone Cabin** (406-682-4253, $35/two, July–Mar.) at the end of a gravel road in the southern end of the Snowcrests. Though Antone has a nearby spring, it's unreliable, and potable water should be brought to all these cabins, which feature propane cooking stoves and outhouses. Antone Cabin can be reached from the Centennial Valley via the Blacktail Creek Road (FS 202), which is an exceptional off-the-beaten-byway gravel route back to Dillon and I-15.

Best Eats

West Yellowstone: Sydney's Mountain Bistro ($$/$$$, 406-646-7660, L/D), **Bullwinkle's Saloon & Eatery** ($$, 406-646-9664/406-646-7974, L/D), and **Ernie's Deli** ($, 406-646-9467, B/L/D) are open year-round. Sydney's, a personal favorite, breaks from what you'd expect and meets gourmet standards; the bistro uses fresh, local ingredients when possible and has an inspired wine list. Bullwinkle's is the place to get messy with baby back ribs but also offers some not-so-standard specialty salads, pan-fried trout, and pasta as well as the ubiquitous beef and bison steaks. They also own a conveniently located liquor/wine/beer store, where you are

Yesterday's Calf-A in Dell, once a pioneer schoolhouse, is a favorite of I-15 travelers for its home-style cookin'.

welcome to choose and purchase a bottle to accompany your meal. Ernie's has eye-opening coffee, sandwiches, salads, and plenty of vegetarian options. For a cup of mindfulness of your surroundings, check out the latest earthquake activity on Ernie's Web site; it will awaken you to the shaky ground beneath your feet. For breakfast, we like the **Running Bear Pancake House** ($/$$, 406-646-7703, B/L), open in the summer and winter but not during the shoulder seasons.

Lima: Jan's Café ($$, 406-276-3484, B/L/D) has been around since the 1960s and is known locally for its pork sausage cowboy burger, not to mention delish deep-dish fruit and cream pies.

Dell: One of the more renowned rural restaurants in Montana—and not just with I-15 truckers—is **Yesterday's Bar and Calf-A** ($/$$, 406-276-3308, B/L/D), 8 miles northwest of Lima on the interstate, which some say is the middle of nowhere. Located in an 1890s redbrick schoolhouse, with its bell and belfry still intact, the Calf-A isn't much for ambience but serves such simple home cookin' as tender beef pot roast alongside a heaping helping of mashed potatoes and homemade pies for dessert…or anytime. Outside seating, with views of the towering Tendoy Mountains, is a summer treat best enjoyed with their old-fashioned doughnuts, maple bars, and cinnamon rolls.

Best Bar

West Yellowstone: Not only does the **Wild West Pizzeria & Saloon** (406-646-7259/406-646-4400) have the best pizza in the area, it's also a lively local hangout. The pizzas—hand tossed, made from Wheat Montana brand flour, and topped with freshly grated Wisconsin mozzarella cheese—take some time to get to your table. But they are so worth the wait and best enjoyed with a local beer and big-screen TV in their handsome, expanded new digs. The bar has a pool table and can get loud, but take your microbrew or wine back to the pine tables and benches for conversation. And here's the bonus with Wild West: It's open year-round.

The Perfect Weekend

Stay your first night at one of the many serviceable lodging options in West Yellowstone and be sure to have supper at the **Bistro**. In the morning, have a heaping portion of pancakes at the **Running Bear Pancake**

House and grab a lunch to go at **Ernie's Deli**. Head out on US 20, stop for an hour of fly-fishing on **Henrys Lake**, and continue on toward Red Rock Pass. Once over the pass, snap a photo of the uppermost headwaters of the Missouri River at the small bridge over Hellroaring Creek. At the junction of Elk Lake Road, turn north to check in for a night at the **Elk Lake Resort**. Continue back to Red Rock Pass Road and look for wildlife while having your deli lunch at the campground just south of Upper Red Rock Lake. Find a game trail and hike into the **Red Rock Lakes National Wildlife Refuge**. At Monida, merge onto I-15 and drive north for dinner at **Yesterday's Bar and Calf-A** in Dell. Return to Elk Lake Resort, either repeating the route to see what you missed or taking North Side Road across the northern part of the valley.

DETOUR: ONE FOR THE ROAD

The Gallatin Canyon

Gallatin Gateway to West Yellowstone

Estimated length: 76 miles

Highlights: Scenic vistas, wildlife viewing, Big Sky, Gallatin Gateway Inn, Yellowstone National Park.

Some of the most beautiful images from *A River Runs Through It* were filmed in this picturesque canyon. For about 65 miles, twisting US 191 separates the Gallatin and Madison ranges, hugging the Gallatin River from the mouth of the canyon just south of Bozeman to within a few miles of the river's genesis in Yellowstone National Park.

The highlight is clearly the scenery, with realistic chances of seeing bear, moose, elk, deer, and bison. In fact, from March to May, when bison are migrating from the park to greener pastures west of US 191, it's imperative to keep a close eye out for the shaggy beasts—especially at night. Most of the drive features steep canyon slopes blanketed in Douglas fir and lodgepole pine, but midway is the congestion of **Big Sky**, a destination resort that sprang from a mountain meadow almost overnight in the mid-1970s. Along the way are periodic guest ranches and steakhouses, all adding to the aura.

A note of caution: The Gallatin Canyon is also one of Montana's most dangerous drives, a sobering reality marked by the steady parade of white crosses flanking the road. Many locals headed to West Yellowstone opt for the broad Madison Valley just to the west instead of negotiating the S-turns in the Gallatin. The traffic has eased some in the down economy, as fewer construction workers are making the twice-daily pilgrimages to build trophy homes for the rich in Big Sky and the ultra-rich at the Yellowstone Club.

US 191 leaves I-90 at Bozeman, but you can also continue to the Belgrade exit 8 miles to the northwest and take Jackrabbit Road south to Four Corners. Continue south toward the mountains and the mouth of the Gallatin Canyon. The most striking feature before the canyon is the **Gallatin Gateway Inn**, an extravagant 42,000-square-foot Spanish-style building constructed in 1927 as a terminus for the Chicago, Milwaukee & St. Paul Railway spur that brought Yellowstone visitors to the area. The inn has 33 well-appointed guest rooms and cottages, and its **Porter House** restaurant is a cut above.

A few miles later, you'll enter the canyon, and the Gallatin immediately changes from a braided, meandering stream to a swift emerald river with solid whitewater stretches. Just past Spanish Creek, look upstream to Storm Castle, a jutting rock formation. Farther along on the left is a fast-paced straight stretch of river known as "The Mad Mile," a favorite of rafters and kayakers when water levels are accommodating in the spring and early summer. The highlight is a giant boulder midstream called House Rock.

Thirty-six miles south of Gallatin Gateway is the only stoplight between Four Corners and West Yellowstone: The junction of MT 64. Two miles up that road is the town of Big Sky, and a few miles past that are **Big Sky Ski Resort**, **Moonlight Basin Ski Area** and **Lone Mountain Ranch**, all popular ski destinations. This area was a picturesque ranch when the late NBC newscaster Chet Huntley, a Montana native, rode in with friends on horseback in the early 1970s, envisioning a destination golf resort. When he saw Lone Mountain rising on the western skyline, his vision changed. There is still golfing aplenty at Big Sky, which features courses designed by former professional stars Arnold Palmer and Tom Weiskopf, a Bozeman resident.

South of Big Sky, the terrain gets wild enough to support populations of grizzly bears and wolves. Aside from an occasional restaurant (**The Corral** is a great beer and burger stop) and a few historic guest ranches (the **320 Ranch** has a well-above-average public restaurant), there aren't as many people on this stretch, though you'll have company from fly fishermen casting to rainbow and cutthroat trout. After Sage Creek, Taylor Fork, and the Elkhorn Ranch, the road enters Yellowstone National Park, where the speed limit drops to 55 mph for the next 25 miles; there is no park fee to drive this stretch. Several trailheads are along US 191 here, including the popular Bighorn and Fawn Pass trails, which join to form a loop in the mountains to the east. If you do hike, bring bear spray, make noise, and, if possible, travel in groups of four or more.

Eventually US 191 leaves the park, crests a hill, and brings into view the broad Madison Valley, carpeted by lodgepole pine. In the winter and spring, chances are good you'll see a bison ambling alongside the road. They are allowed to remain outside the park until mid-May, when Montana's Department of Livestock chases them back. Long straight-aways subsequently lead into the town of West Yellowstone.

Remnants of Parrot Castle, an old mining facility, rise above the Jefferson River.

CHAPTER

3

Ghost Towns and Living History: The Vigilante Trail

Three Forks to Cardwell

Estimated length: 118 miles
Estimated time: 3 hours to 2 days

Highlights: Missouri Headwaters State Park, Norris Hot Springs, Madison River, Virginia City, Nevada City, garnet mines, Parrot Castle, Renova Hot Springs, Lewis and Clark Caverns State Park.

Getting there: Because a small section of this loop parallels I-90, there are several options: Leave the interstate at Whitehall and head south on MT 55 toward Twin Bridges, get off at Cardwell and drive toward Whitehall or La Hood, and exit at US 287 just west of Three Forks, or start your tour at the Three Forks exit with a visit to Missouri Headwaters State Park. Coming from the east, you might even leave I-90 at Bozeman and follow US 191 down Main Street through Four Corners to Norris. Regardless, leave plenty of time because few routes pack more unique adventures into 120 miles than this one.

Overview

Think Montana mining history, and the yawning holes in the earth around Butte and Anaconda may come to mind. To reach farther back into Montana mining lore—back to the pick-and-shovel days—ply the Vigilante Trail, which has no fewer than six ghost towns within its circumference.

The drive surrounds the stately Tobacco Root Mountains, which are littered with rusting mining equipment easily rediscovered by hikers ascending to the range's sparkling alpine lakes. The ghost towns of Pony, which is still active, and Mammoth, which isn't active, are in this deceptively burly mountain range.

The fulcrum of this route is colorful Virginia City, the Williamsburg of the West. Once a rootin'-tootin' territorial capital that was the largest city in the Inland Northwest after the Civil War, today "VC" boasts the oldest functioning county courthouse in Montana amid authentic buildings still doing business—albeit mostly for tourists. Virginia City is at the eastern and uppermost end of what 150 years ago was dubbed "Fourteen-Mile City" because the community stretched for 14 miles along Alder Gulch to present-day Alder. As you drive between Virginia City and Alder on MT 287, you'll notice mile after mile and pile after pile of rounded river rock along Alder Creek as if a backhoe were breaking ground for a long strip mall. These are the remnants of placer mining, which entails collecting gold nuggets and flakes on the surface—as opposed to hard-rock mining, where shafts or open pits are dug to reach veins underground. The mounds are a result of using hydraulic jets to separate gold from dirt and rocks, a high-tech form of mining that replaced the less-intrusive but less-effective gold pans. The Alder Gulch placer mines produced more gold than any other region in the Northwest. Because of this prosperity, Virginia City had 1,200 buildings and the first school and newspaper in the territory.

The area wasn't just about mining, though. Before railroad spurs were built to West Yellowstone and Gallatin Gateway, Virginia City was the hub of traffic to Yellowstone National Park. By 1875, as the mines began playing out and settlers migrated, the capital was moved to Helena. The town rapidly began losing population and fell into disrepair until the 1940s, when a family named Bovey bought much of what remained and began restoration. The entire city became a National Historic Landmark in 1961 and has a multitude of street-side plaques to prove it.

After spending an afternoon or longer walking the wood planks of Virginia City and absorbing all the activities, you might be inclined to take a passing nod at what appears to be little more than a collection of dilapidated frontier buildings and speed right through the blinking yellow light in Nevada City. We advise against it. In many ways, Nevada City captures the essence of Montana's frontier mining legacy even more than Virginia City and it is a museum unto itself. There are 14 original buildings here; the remainder, thanks in great measure to the Boveys, were rescued from just about every corner of the state, including a saddlery from the Indian agency in Fort Benton that the celebrated western artist C. M. Russell frequented.

But there's much, much more to this route. The Madison River at fly-fishing-centric Ennis is a world-famous trout stream, and the four rivers converging near the appealing community of Twin Bridges aren't far behind in their angling prowess. The Lewis and Clark Caverns State Park features the most extensive and accessible labyrinth of limestone caves in the Northern Rockies. Two hot springs, Norris and Renova, offer contrasting experiences—one primitively developed, the other just primitive. And then there's Three Forks, with its cornerstone white and pillared hotel—a choice spot to unwind after a day exploring the site where the mighty Missouri River begins its journey to St. Louis upon collecting the waters of the Madison, Jefferson, and Gallatin rivers.

Hitting the Road

Where to begin? We suggest **Three Forks** (pop. 1,728), a mostly blue-collar community whose economy is tied to agriculture and a talc plant. The most impressive landmark is **The Sacajawea Hotel**, which had its first heyday around the turn of the previous century. That's when passengers were dropped at the Milwaukee Road railway station across the street and rested at the hotel for a carriage ride to Yellowstone. Three Forks' fate changed irreversibly when the railroad extended a spur farther south to Gallatin Gateway, and now the old station is a Chinese restaurant. But the 100-year-old hotel, now owned and lovingly refurbished by the Folkvord family of Wheat Montana renown, is breathing living history into the community.

Before leaving Three Forks, wander the trails and read the interpretive signs at the 532-acre **Missouri Headwaters State Park** (406-285-3610). Each summer evening features speakers who recount stories, including Lewis and Clark camping at the confluence of the three rivers and the Shoshone woman Sacagawea's capture by Hidatsa Indians when she was 13. Heading southwest of Three Forks on US 287/MT 2 west of the Jefferson River, the sod-roofed **Parker Homestead** is still standing on the west side of the highway even though in 2010 Montana Fish, Wildlife & Parks dropped its smallest park from the system.

Where MT 2 and US 287 split near Sappington Bridge over the Jefferson, veer south on 287 toward **Harrison** (pop. 162). Agricultural lands

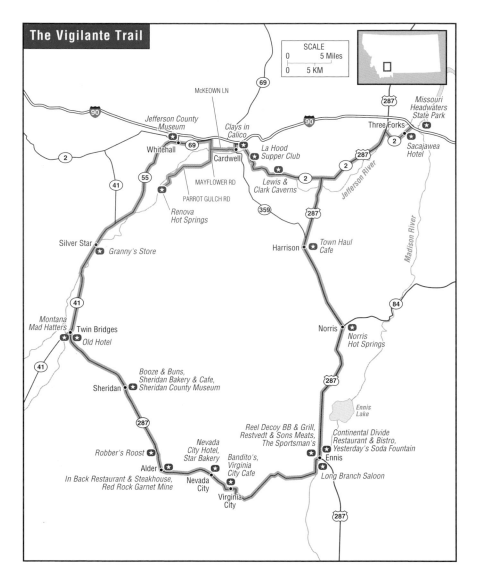

The Vigilante Trail

SCALE
0   5 Miles
0   5 KM

McKEOWN LN

Missouri
Headwaters
State Park

Jefferson County
Museum

Clays in
Calico

Three Forks

Whitehall

Sacajawea
Hotel

Cardwell

La Hood
Supper Club

Lewis &
Clark Caverns

Jefferson River

MAYFLOWER RD

PARROT GULCH RD

Renova
Hot Springs

Madison River

Silver Star

Granny's Store

Harrison

Town Haul
Cafe

Montana
Mad Hatters

Twin Bridges

Old Hotel

Norris

Norris
Hot Springs

Booze & Buns,
Sheridan Bakery & Cafe,
Sheridan County Museum

Sheridan

Ennis
Lake

Reel Decoy BB & Grill,
Restvedt & Sons Meats,
The Sportsman's

Continental Divide
Restaurant & Bistro,
Yesterday's Soda Fountain

Nevada
City Hotel,
Star Bakery

Robber's Roost

Bandito's,
Virginia
City Cafe

Ennis

Alder

Long Branch Saloon

In Back Restaurant & Steakhouse,
Red Rock Garnet Mine

Nevada
City

Virginia
City

begin to give way to sagebrush steppe as you continue another 12 miles
south to **Norris** (pop. 109), which is little more than a wide junction in
the road with a gas station, biker bar, and hit-and-miss Mexican restaurant housed in an old schoolhouse. Most people hurry through from Bozeman to Ennis, but 1 mile east on MT 84 is a rejuvenated and family-friendly
Norris Hot Springs (406-685-3303), aka "Water of the Gods." Norris lures
locals and tourists in the know for a soak, good eats from a predominantly
locally sourced menu, and live music played from a geodome stage on

weekends. The intimate pool is emptied and filled daily, but closed on Mondays and Tuesdays for a thorough scrubbing.

South of Norris, US 287 climbs over a modest pass, revealing majestic views of the Tobacco Root, Gravelly, and Madison mountains above Ennis Lake and the famous Madison Valley. Although the Madison River is a fisherman's paradise from source to mouth, a brisk stretch above **Ennis** (pop. 840), reverently called the 50-Mile Riffle, is famous for its lunker rainbow and brown trout. That Ennis caters to these anglers is obvious from the large sculpture of a fly fisherman in a small plaza at the junction of US 287 and MT 287. For some munchies or tasty Montana souvenirs to take home, **Restvedt & Son Meat Market** (406-682-7306) is renowned for its bison and beef jerky and smoked meats. From Ennis, head right on MT 287, which curls south and begins rising to a sage steppe divide between the Tobacco Roots on the north and Gravellys to the south. After driving past clusters of ranchettes, stop at one of the overlooks and take a sweeping last look at the Madison Valley, with the Madison Range as a dramatic backdrop. Looking due east, you'll see treeless Blaze and Lone mountains; to the south is a square-jawed and isolated geologic buttress called Sphinx Mountain. Once at the summit, you'll immediately begin the winding drop toward **Virginia City** (pop. 132). Most of the historic buildings are on the main drag, Wallace Street, west of Broadway. Virginia City and **Nevada City** both provide informative tabloid-shaped handouts during tourist season for walking tours. Park in Virginia City and get a different view of both towns by taking the narrow-gauge **Alder Gulch Short Line Railroad** (406-843-5247) to Nevada City and back. The train operates Memorial Day Weekend through mid-September and leaves on the hour.

A requisite of visiting Virginia City is to take in one—or both—of the town's lively entertainment offerings. The **Opera House** (406-843-5314, May–Sept.) is home to the state's oldest professional acting company, the Virginia City Players, who perform classic family-oriented vaudeville Tuesdays through Sundays. In the original Gilbert Brewery building is the more tawdry **Brewery Follies** (406-843-5218/800-829-2969, May–Sept.), which offers mostly blue humor that can turn even a ghost's face red. Speaking of ghosts, tours of the town's many haunted buildings are offered at 9 PM each night in the summer.

Unlike its neighboring city, where folks still work and play amid living history, Nevada City is a sprawling open-air museum. Rusted mining equipment is scattered about crumbling railroad cars on the south side of

Rusting railroad cars and mining equipment line the tracks on the Alder Gulch Short Line Railroad.

MT 287. On the north side, the Boveys have put together an entire community of wooden structures, accessed between the Music Hall and Dry Goods Store. If some of the buildings look vaguely familiar, perhaps it's because scenes from *Little Big Man, The Missouri Breaks,* and other western movies were filmed here. The town features daily reenactments during the summer, with people dressed in the garb of the 1860s. Try to see the two-story outhouse, gallows barn where a triple hanging took place, and China Town—a tribute to an often-exploited but nevertheless invaluable culture of the American West.

Departing Nevada City to the west on MT 287, the placer mounds along the creek become more pronounced as you get closer to a blip of blacktop called **Alder** (pop. 106), the railroad terminus for all the mining equipment transported to the gulch. Right before you enter town you'll find **Red Rock Garnet Mine** (406-842-5760), where you can pan for gold or try your luck digging for gems. You're now in the mistakenly named **Ruby Valley**, so dubbed because when garnets were discovered they were confused for rubies. If trout fishing is your gig, the Ruby River below Ruby Dam is great for wading or bank fishing. Much of the Ruby flows through private land, but there are four fishing access sites south of town, and you're allowed to ply any stretch of a Montana river as long as you stay below the normal high-water mark. At Alder, MT 287 bends north through **Laurin** (La-Ray), a ghost town of sorts that has a **Hangman's Tree**, the stately limestone **St. Mary of the Assumption** gothic-style church, and the abandoned two-story **Robber's Roost** roadhouse on the left side of the highway. At Robber's Roost, you can read the story of stagecoach travelers between Virginia City and Bannack who were robbed and terrorized by so-called road agents.

This is the heart of the Garnet, er, Ruby Valley, with **Sheridan** (pop. 659) as its peaceful hub. The **Sheridan County Museum** (406-287-3605) opened in a spacious new building in 2006 and remains a work-in-progress, but it offers a nice snapshot of the county's history. From Sheridan, the valley broadens to accommodate the convergence of the Ruby, Beaverhead, and Big Hole rivers at **Twin Bridges** (pop. 400), where Lewis and Clark camped two centuries ago. Bicycle-friendly Twin Bridges, which bills itself as "The Town That Cares," has a lot going on for a community with one blinking-light intersection. This is the home of the world-famous **R.L. Winston Rod Co.** (406-684-5674), which has produced coveted bamboo and graphite fly rods since the company moved from San Francisco in the mid-1970s; tours are offered weekdays. Downtown, take a gander at **Montana Mad Hatters** (406-684-5869), where Cowboy Hall of Fame inductee Sheila Kirkpatrick-Masse has been making custom cowboy hats since she was a teenager, when she made one to fit her personality. Visit just to see the authentic collection of tattered, trampled, and sweat-streaked cowboy hats donated by area ranchers. One curiosity on the western edge of town is a group of weathered brick buildings that looks like a small college campus. This is the abandoned state orphanage.

MT 287 ends in Twin Bridges. Go straight through the intersection on MT 41, which follows the Jefferson River north between the Tobacco Roots on the east and Highland Mountains on the west. Ten miles up the road is little **Silver Star** (pop. 98), marked by a highway sign and a fenced collection of privately owned railroad cabooses and retired mining equipment—including five giant wheel-shaped pieces hauled out of a defunct mine at Butte. Across the highway is **Granny's Store** (406-287-3605), which has the usual sundries complemented by an extraordinary collection of mostly regional books. Four miles north of Silver Star, veer right onto MT 55 toward **Whitehall** (pop. 1,044), whose primary industry is evident in the gaping mountainside gash straight ahead—the Golden Sunlight gold mine. Although our route takes you around Whitehall, one reason to pass through is to see 10 brightly colored **Lewis & Clark Murals** generally near the intersection of First Avenue and Division Street. Local artist Kit Mather has put journal entries from the expedition into a detailed picture format. On the south side of town is the free **Jefferson Valley Museum** (406-287-7813, summers), located in a bright red barn and featuring exhibits honoring NBC's Huntley, who grew up here.

It isn't difficult to deduce the favorite summer pastime in Twin Bridges.

Heading through Whitehall, just before reaching I-90 turn east on MT 2/69 toward **Cardwell** (pop. 40). About halfway between the towns, head off the beaten byway on Mayflower Road. Cross the Jefferson River and backtrack to the west on Parrot Gulch Road. After several miles, a mysterious round brick structure rises to the west of the gravel road. A few feet beyond, the remains of **Parrot Castle**, once part of an old mining community and now a river access point, open up at your feet. Continuing on a few hundred yards up the road, the Tobacco Roots foothills meet the river at Point of Rocks. In a side channel of the river is an inviting geothermal hot spot known as **Renova Hot Springs**. It's about 10 feet below the road and one of the few undeveloped thermal areas in Montana suitable for soaking. There are two pools identified by the sulfur odor and rock rings built by soakers; the best time to take in nature's hot tub is summer and fall, when river levels are down and water temperatures are ideal. From the springs, reverse course, recross the Mayflower Bridge, and turn west on MT 2 toward Cardwell. At the T junction a mile south of Cardwell, stop at **Clays in Calico** (406-287-3498), which calls itself the oldest pottery house in the state and crafts all of its vessels from Montana clay.

Before reaching the interstate in Cardwell, turn east on MT 2. The highway follows a railroad past a wide spot in the road called **La Hood** and into a short serpentine canyon carved by the Jefferson. Once out of the canyon, you'll arrive at the entrance for **Lewis and Clark Caverns State Park** (406-287-3541/406-287-3032), a must on any itinerary unless claustrophobia is an issue. Montana's first state park offers camping, picnicking, and hiking year-round. But the primary attraction—the largest collection of limestone caves in the Northwest—is only available by guided tour May 1 through September 30. Park at the visitors center and hike the 3 miles from the dusty sage into the pines to the gift shop and information center, or drive to the top parking lot where there is also a small snack and souvenir stand. The tours take two hours and are a window into a fantastic world of stalagmites, stalactites, bats, and other underground curiosities. There are some tight quarters, including the Beaver Slide, where you must either waddle, limbo, or slide on your derriere through a narrow gap, but the experience is too good to pass up. The park also offers Friday night campfire programs and naturalist talks during summers.

After leaving the caverns on MT 2, you'll pass a large area on the left that looks like an F Troop stockade with an old railroad bridge out front. This is the site of the **Rockin' the River Festival**, a wildly popular outdoor

concert held every August that has featured the likes of Alice Cooper, For-
eigner, REO Speedwagon, Steppenwolf, among other famed rock bands.
You'll shortly rejoin US 287 about 10 miles southwest of Three Forks,
where you can close the day where it began—at the Sacajawea Hotel.

Best Places to Bunk

Three Forks: To begin the loop fully refreshed, spend at least one night
in **The Sacajawea Hotel** ($$/$$$, 406-285-6515). The 29 rooms under-
went a multimillion-dollar facelift in 2010, providing some of the best
sleeping comfort in the state.

Ennis: Fishermen park their Orvis rods and Simms waders at the leg-
endary and immaculately landscaped **El Western Motel** ($$, 406-682-
4217/800-831-2773) south of town on the east bank of the river. The El
Western is also a family favorite with its setting and collection of cabins
and lodges befitting a picture postcard from the 1950s. **The Sportsman's
Lodge** ($/$$, 406-682-4242) is a compact complex of 19 lodgepole log
cabins and 11 motel units north of the junction of MT 287; it has a
priced-right restaurant as well that's popular for good reason.

Virginia City: To get the true feel of an old West experience, stay at the
creaky **Fairweather Inn** ($$, 800-829-2969, May–Sept.). The amenities in
its 15 rooms only slightly surpass those of a prosperous yesteryear. The
Carriage House ($$, 406-843-5211), a studio apartment with a kitch-
enette, and the **Cozy Cabin** ($$, 406-843-5211), are open year-round; the
cabin is centrally located and has received contemporary upgrades while
retaining its mining-days feel. **The Stonehouse Inn** ($$, 406-843-5504,
May–Sept.), an 1884 Gothic revival home, includes a full breakfast.

Nevada City: The **Nevada City Hotel** ($$, 800-829-2969, May–Sept.),
owned by John and Linda Hamilton, proprietors of the Fairweather and
Stonehouse, was carted over from near Twin Bridges; parts were
reclaimed from an old employee dorm in Yellowstone, and its uneven
floors and creaky doors give away its authenticity. Behind the hotel are
17 actual pioneer cabins—numbered 1 to 18, superstitiously skipping
number 13—gathered from around Montana, including two from
Nevada City. **Just An Experience Bed & Breakfast** ($$$, 406-843-5402)
has lush cabins, lodge rooms, and a mining museum to boot.

Spend a night in one of the original miners' cabins behind the Nevada City Hotel.

Alder: Accommodations are limited, but **Chick's Motel & R/V Park** ($, 406-842-5366) is clean and has drive-to-your-door rooms at economy rates.

Laurin: Vigilante and road-agent history notwithstanding, you'll feel perfectly safe and comfortable at the economical **Elijah's Rest** ($$, 406-842-7295, May–Nov.), which has three externally similar but internally unique log cabins. Included is a full breakfast highlighted by Elijah's biscuits and gravy.

Sheridan: The sparkling new nine-room **Happy Trails Inn** ($/$$, 406-842-5797) has to be one of the few inns in America fashioned from a bowling alley. It has a spalike look and feel, a bit unusual for the sur-roundings, but it's a real find. Far more historic is the stately **Victorian Ruby Valley Inn** ($$, 406-842-7111), comprising four suites geared to gentrified anglers wanting to cast a fly in one of the nearby streams.

Twin Bridges: The Old Hotel ($$/$$$, 406-684-5959) is just that—a ren-ovated 1879 three-story brick hotel with two well-appointed guest suites above a knock-your-waders-off restaurant.

Alternative Bunking

Ennis: Usually full in the summer are both the **Camper Corner** (406-682-4514) in the heart of town and **Ennis RV Village** (406-682-1463) north of town, both with full hookups and sites for tenters. For a country lake experience, the **Lake Shore Cabins & Campground** (406-682-4424, May–Nov.) on the north side of Ennis Lake has RV and tent sites, a studio apartment, four-bedroom house, and marina; three-night minimum.

Virginia City: The **Virginia City RV Park** (406-843-5493), on the left just as you enter the east end of town, has wireless Internet, showers, a free RV dump station for guests, and is pet friendly.

Alder: Our pick would be the **KOA Kabins** (406-842-5677), aka Two Ed KOA, sprinkled among well-groomed campsites surrounded by conspicu-ous evidence of placer mining. Two Eds are better than one: One Ed owns it, the other Ed—nicknamed Gunny—manages it. Ed the owner calls it the "fin, fur, and feather capital of the world." The campground is known to, what Ed calls, the "high-speed guys, steak and lobster eaters" for its comfort and friendliness.

Twin Bridges: The smallish **Stardust Country Inn & RV Park** (406-684-5648) has nine RV sites and six spots for tenters.

Silver Star: About 2 miles south of town, fishing is the focus at the 75-acre **Jefferson River Camp** (406-684-5225), which has 14 RV sites and eight places for tenters. The camp has a half mile of private river access and features guided fishing trips from the Four Rivers Fly Shop. There's also a cabin and an apartment.

Cardwell: Lewis and Clark Caverns State Park (406-287-3541) not only has 40 camp sites and three basic camping cabins that sleep up to four, it also offers the unique chance to stay in a teepee. The cabins are similar to those at KOA campgrounds—bring your own bedding.

Camping: The Beaverhead-Deerlodge National Forest has four primitive but free campgrounds in the Tobacco Root Mountains—three in the Mill Creek drainage accessible from Sheridan on the west side and one on South Willow Creek on the east side near the head of the Potosi Trail, a popular way to access the mountains' many glistening alpine lakes. **Potosi** has 15 sites and two water pumps. The three on the west side are **Mill Creek** (nine sites), **Balanced Rock** (two), and **Branham Lakes** (13); Branham is the highest in elevation and has potable water, as does Mill Creek.

Best Eats

Three Forks: The elegant **Pompey's Grill** ($$/$$$, 406-285-6515, D, Wed.–Sun.) or the more casual **Sacajawea Bar** ($, 406-285-6515, D) in the Sacajawea Hotel are worth any drive. The grill has set the bar for gourmet dining with its energetic Chef Matt, who brings a big-city flair to a small town. Favored items on the menu, which changes seasonally, include the 20-ounce "One Big Ass Steak," wild sockeye salmon topped with avocado lime vinaigrette, bison short ribs braised in Moose Drool beer, and the ultimate comfort food—macaroni and cheese made with three cheeses, smoked bacon, and chicken. Salads are complemented with house-made dressings that are beyond the ordinary and accompanied by signature dinner rolls with herbed butter.

Harrison: The **Town Haul Café** ($/$$, 406-685-3207, B/L/D), formerly Café 287, uses local meat (the beef is raised by the owner's husband), potatoes, and salad greens and serves up homemade soups, pies, and classic cinnamon rolls. The quirky name is a nod to the truckers who always have the cafe on their US 287 itineraries.

Ennis: This fly-fishing Mecca enjoys a plethora of solid eating establishments befitting a tourist destination, most open only seasonally, however. Even the well-stocked local supermarket, **Madison Foods** ($, 406-682-4306), packs an angler lunch to go. **Sunrise Bagels** ($, 406-682-7900, B/L), usually open except in the dead of winter, has the best bagels west of the Big Apple. Enjoy an old-fashioned malted or cool ice-cream treat after a satisfying hot sandwich at **Yesterday's Soda Fountain** ($, 406-682-7568,

B/L). Exceptional value can be found at **The Sportsman's** ($$/$$$, 406-682-4242, B/L/D) in the form of classic steak Diane, Parmesan halibut in Dijon sauce, or green curry noodles and veggies. On the west side of town, gnaw on some smoked ribs or chicken, fresh farm-raised trout, or a vegetarian delight at the always busy yet friendly **Reel Decoy BBQ & Grill** ($$, 406-682-3858, B/L/D); it's open May through November. Or if you're in the mood for a gourmet meal paired with a fine wine, the trendy and spendy **Continental Divide Restaurant** ($$$, 406-682-7600, D) will fill the void, as long as you're there between May and mid-October.

Virginia City: Housed in the Wells Fargo building, **Bandito's** ($$$, 406-843-5556, B/L/D) has a savory mix of Montana-Mex entrées from Memorial Day through Labor Day weekend and hosts five to six summer concerts with national and local acts. The **Virginia City Café** ($/$$, 406-843-5311, L/D), open summers, adjoins the town's watering hole, the **Pioneer Bar** ($, 406-843-5550, L/D). The café is a personal favorite for its "scratch" cookin' and perfectly grilled elk-bison burger served with a pile of kitchen-made fries.

Nevada City: Under passionate new ownership in 2010, the **Star Bakery** ($, 406-843-5525, B/L/D) is in one of Nevada City's 14 original buildings (1863) and a weekend destination during the summer season for its eggs Benedict (Sundays), four-spice pancakes, "fruits of the forest" pies, and fried pickles.

Alder: Behind Chick's Bar and across the parking lot from the motel is **In Back Restaurant & Steakhouse** ($$, 406-842-7632, B/L/D), decorated in contemporary John Deere and serving tractor-tire-sized burgers and Sunday night prime-rib specials.

Sheridan: The best-known stop is the **Sheridan Bakery & Café** ($, 406-843-3715, B/L) for baked goods and heaping breakfasts that run under $8. Equally impressive is the new **Booze & Buns** ($, 406-842-5790) with its 380 wine labels, well-stocked liquor shelves, and a selection of coffee and tasty pastries to get your giddy up—cinnamon rolls, sticky buns, streudel, scones, and muffins.

Twin Bridges: Generally considered to have the best traditional dinner in the area, the **Blue Anchor** ($$/$$$, 406-684-5655, D) is easily recognized by its powder-blue exterior, large neon anchor sign and blue Naugahyde-covered chairs. Hungry cyclists or cowhands can dive into burgers, steaks, or seafood during the spring and summer; the bar is open year-round but doesn't serve food. For an equally enticing but entirely different dining experience, the **Old Hotel** ($$$, 406-684-5959, Sunday brunch/D) boasts an international, ever-changing menu with such highlights as Thai pork kabobs, tyro pitas, unusual soups (apple walnut if you're lucky), and, to cap if off, homemade sorbet. The Old Hotel is open year-round, but hours are irregular. For casual dining, **The Shack** ($/$$, 406-684-5050, L/D) has hand-tossed pizzas, salads, sandwiches, and cold brews. Grab a cuppa joe and eats-to-go at the **Jumping Rainbow Espresso** ($, 406-4684-5222, B/L) from the queen of "eat local," Sarah Miller. (We're hooked on her chai shake sweetened with local honey.)

Nevada City's Star Bakery is renowned for its eggs Benedict, served only on Sunday.

La Hood: The historic **La Hood Park Supper Club** ($$/$$$, 406-287-3281, L/D) has credible hand-cut steaks, seafood and baby back ribs, served amid a backdrop of local western paintings, but summer floaters on the Jefferson River know the best reason to stop is for a memorable margarita and to chat up Steve while his wife does her chef thing.

Best Bars

Ennis: Truth be told, there is many a friendly bar stool waiting along this route, making it difficult to designate "the best." If we must narrow it down to, say, two, our choices would be the **Long Branch Saloon** in Ennis, which barely edges its sister bar, the **Claim Jumper Saloon**, simply because we've had more fun at the Long Branch. Both are classic western saloons where the old-timers mix with tourists, anglers, seasonal residents, and even the semifamous. Karaoke nights at the Long Branch are a hoot.

Three Forks: The newly renovated **Sacajawea Bar** in the basement of the hotel offers a fresh place to stretch or take a drink out to the long front porch. Shoot pool, watch a game on the big screen, play poker, or, on weekends, dance to live music. The Sac Bar's menu has a little something for everyone, but don't miss the homemade kettle chips.

Virginia City: The dark and musty **Pioneer Bar** doesn't do much dressing up; it isn't necessary. The walls are cluttered with historical artifacts, including a bison wall mount with a plaque telling the sad saga of a shaggy beast that once roamed the prairies by the tens of millions. During the summer you can order from the Virginia City Café's menu; the rest of the year, treat yourself to a Bob's Pizza.

3-7-77 INSTILLED FEAR IN LAWLESS MONTANANS

Look closely and you'll see the numbers 3-7-77 in some interesting places: on the shoulder patches of members of the Montana Highway Patrol, on the jumpsuits of Montana Air National Guard pilots, and, most revealing, above the front entrance to the historic Robber's Roost roadhouse outside Laurin. The origin of these numbers has always been a mystery, but in the late 1870s and early 1880s everyone in Montana's gold country knew what they represented: vigilante justice.

The numbers were a reference to an 1860s gang that hunted down thieving road agents and hanged them without trials. As the vigilante legend has grown over the years, the story goes that if the numbers appeared in the middle of the night on a man's cabin, he knew he had precious little time to get out of Dodge—precisely 3 hours, 7 minutes, and 77 seconds, according to some local lore. Officially, this method of law enforcement was frowned upon, but it's understandable why lawmen looked the other way. After all, for a time rowdy Alder Gulch area was as crime-free as anyplace in Montana.

Thing is, history and legend don't quite align. The vigilantes' heyday was in 1864, when within five weeks they rode through a number of mining camps and hanged 21 ne'er-do-wells, one being a local sheriff. Such thirst for this unique brand of frontier justice continued until about 1870, when a combination of the arrival of new residents via train and the departure of miners for the gold in the Black Hills briefly led to a kinder, gentler society.

It wasn't until 1879, though, after the unexplained murder of a Helena businessman led the town's newspaper editor to call for vengeance and the rebirth of 1864 vigilante justice, that the numbers 3-7-77 first appeared, all in conspicuous locations around the capital city.

Though careful study has shown the numbers have no relation to the actual vigilantes of the 1860s, the two are inextricably linked in history, and today the numbers are a symbol of Montana law enforcement. The word *vigilante* remains popular in Montana, where it appears on a sports stadium, a rodeo's name, and a popular theater group's marquis.

Speculation about the meaning of the numbers makes for great debate today. Having 3 hours, 7 minutes, and 77 seconds to leave town makes for a great tale of explanation, but there's even a better one—3-7-77 are the dimensions of a thief's grave.

Perfect Weekend

Start your Friday night in Three Forks with dinner at **Pompey's Grill** and a night at the **Sacajawea Hotel**. Grab breakfast at the **Town Haul Café** in Harrison on the way to spending the morning fishing the **Madison River**. Have lunch at the **Reel Decoy BBQ & Grill** in Ennis and then continue on to **Virginia City** and **Nevada City**. Take the **Alder Gulch Short Line Railroad** from Virginia City to Nevada City and wander amid the historic buildings there. Return to Virginia City via the railroad and pick up tickets to the **Brewery Follies** before having dinner at **Bandito's** and checking into the **Fairweather Inn** for the night. Start your morning with breakfast at the **Star Bakery** in Nevada City and then mosey on to Twin Bridges to check out all the area ranchers' cowboy hats at **Montana Mad Hatters**. Stop for lunch at **The Shack** in Twin Bridges, and then save the remainder of the afternoon for exploring the cave at **Lewis and Clark Caverns State Park**. Finish with a light dinner at the **Sacajawea Bar** in the hotel in Three Forks.

DETOUR: ONE FOR THE ROAD

The Madison Valley

Ennis to West Yellowstone

Estimated length: 91 miles

Highlights: Madison River, Ennis Lake, Quake Lake, Hebgen Lake.

Getting there: Leave I-90 at Three Forks and take US 287 south to Ennis, or exit in Bozeman, drive south on US 191 to Four Corners, head west on MT 84 to Norris, and turn south on US 287 over the pass through McAllister to Ennis.

Want to see a fly fisherman genuflect? Just mention the Madison River. As American trout streams go, none has more cache among anglers. And although the entire 100-plus miles of the Madison provide excellent fishing, it's the 50-Mile Riffle above Ennis that graces the covers of fly-fishing brochures and fills with drift boats for eight months of the year.

The Madison Valley is broad and sweeping, with US 287 roughly paralleling the river, though usually from a distance. The route has numerous river-access points. And if you don't have a driftboat or raft, there are sections above and below the riffle suited for wading. At McAllister, just north of Ennis, a dirt road goes east to the dam backing up Ennis Lake; below the dam is terrific brown and rainbow trout water. Just below Quake Lake, at the upper end of the valley, is a wading-friendly stretch marked by Three Dollar Bridge, so-named for the toll once charged to cross there.

There are other reasons to be in the Madison Valley, of course—most of them related to outdoor activities and scenery. At Cameron, a road goes east toward the Madison Range and a trailhead that leads to 10,876-foot Sphinx Mountain, the prominent peak whose name requires no explanation.

The farther up the valley you go, the narrower it gets, and the sparkling river comes into view. Off to the left is 11,292-foot Hilgard Peak, second only to Lone Mountain as the tallest in the Madison Range. Eventually the highway begins to bend toward the east. Look for the turnoff across Three Dollar Bridge to Cliff and Wade lakes, part of a string of jewels just over the hill that feature outstanding fishing and the rustic **Wade Lake Resort** cabins (one of our favorite getaways).

Back on US 287, you'll pass MT 87 and drive past an attractive collection of summer homes into Madison Canyon. Immediately coming into view is one of the most unique geologic features in southwest Montana: **Quake Lake.** Looking up on the south, you'll see where in August 1959 an earthquake registering 7.3 on the Richter scale sent 80 million tons of rock and debris into the river and up the other side of the valley. Twenty-eight people died—many remain buried in the rubble—and the slide created a natural dam that formed Quake Lake. The eerie bleached spires of drowned pine trees still poke through the lake's surface. You can walk to the site of the natural dam, which was breached not long after the quake to avoid a future dam break that might imperil residents and fishermen downstream. Stop at the **Earthquake Lake Visitor Center**, where you can read more about the events of August 17, 1959, and possibly even meet a survivor, John Owen, a summer volunteer.

Upstream is man-made **Hebgen Lake**, a boating and fishing favorite. Along the north shore of the lake, the **Hebgen Lake Mountain Inn** is a comfortable place to put your feet up for the night, and the **Happy Hour Bar & Restaurant** has deceivingly good dining for a place with a well-earned, raunchy reputation. In a few miles, US 287 meets up with US 191 for the 9-mile drive into the town of West Yellowstone. (See Gallatin Gateway to West Yellowstone in Chapter 2.)

Rest your motor for the night at Biker's Sanctuary, located in a restored church high above the main drag in Philipsburg.

Montana's Gold, Silver, and Copper Standard: The Anaconda-Pintler Scenic Route

Butte to Drummond

Estimated length: 88 miles
Estimated time: 3 hours to 2 days

Highlights: Museums, hot springs, Berkeley Pit, Old Works Golf Club, Georgetown Lake, Philipsburg, Discovery Ski Basin, Ohrmann Museum & Gallery, Grant-Kohrs Ranch.

Getting there: The Anaconda-Pintler Scenic Route begins and ends at I-90 in southwest Montana. From the east, leave the freeway at the Anaconda-Opportunity turnoff (Exit 208) about 15 miles west of Butte and continue for another 6 miles to Anaconda. From the west, take Exit 155 off I-90 at the little ranch and railroad town of Drummond and head south along Flint Creek.

Overview

Montana's prolific mining past comes to life along much of this drive through thick conifer forests around one of the state's brawniest mountain ranges. The forests are so thick here that it's hard to imagine you're surrounded by the wild shoulders of the Flint Creek Range, which rises to nearly 11,000 feet. Just as prominent as the mountains is the mining history, which fills your windshield the moment you turn off I-90 at Anaconda. A ghostly smelter stack—the tallest man-made structure in Montana—rises

Telltale tailings at the Berkeley Pit in Butte point to the town's mining glory days.
Donna Mitchell

from the mouth of Dutchman Creek. In its heyday, Anaconda was a gritty town of rugged Irish-Catholics whose fortunes ebbed and flowed with the production of copper and gold from the cavernous mines at nearby Butte. This area once produced more copper than any place in the world.

The mines having played out three decades ago, today the communities along the Anaconda-Pintler route are reinventing themselves as tourist towns exploiting their unique histories. The same holds true for Philipsburg, which has become an enclave of museums and theaters celebrating a lively past. Midway through the journey is Georgetown Lake, popular for fishing, snowmobiling, and summer cabins.

Once upon a time, Butte was a collection of ethnic communities—

Italians, Austrians, Finns, Slavs, Mexicans, and, of course, Irish—where grimy workers poked underground for gold and silver in a mile-high bowl west of the Continental Divide. With the advent of electricity came the need for copper, and large quantities were excavated in the late 1800s. By the early 1900s, the population had swelled to more than 100,000 hard-working, hard-drinking, hard-brawling residents who spent their paychecks on booze and brothels in an area of town called "The Line." The landscape literally changed in the mid-1950s, when the Anaconda Copper Mining Company dug the massive **Berkeley Pit** for which Butte is renowned. Entire communities vanished under the toxic slag.

Mining in the giant hole lasted for about three decades, until the 1980s, when operations ceased. Since then, the Berkeley Pit has been filling with toxic water. For a time it appeared that not even Our Lady of the Rockies, a bleached 90-foot-high lighted statue that stands guard over the city from a high mountain atop East Ridge, could save a declining city. Yet Butte somehow endures and perseveres, and today it's capitalizing on its past with popular uptown tours. It's now one of the largest National Historic Landmark Districts in the nation—and it even makes money charging tourists to look into the giant hole.

Hitting the Road

This scenic route starts in Anaconda in the state's eyes, but we suggest you start in **Butte** (pop. 33,892)—a town so proud of its mining origins, ethnicity, and grit that it has its own license plates that state, immodestly, "Butte America." Once the butt of old FBI jokes and derided as the ugliest city this side of Gary, Indiana, today this brick-and mortar town, rising to the lip of the gaping Berkeley Pit and sprinkled with classic mining head frames, emits a certain raw character and leathery charm.

Places to see while in Butte: The **Copper King Mansion** (406-782-7580, May–Sept.) guided tour, **World Museum of Mining** (406-723-7211), and **Mineral Museum** (406-496-4172). For a glimpse of Butte's rambunctious past, don green garb and be there on St. Patrick's Day, when 30,000 residents and visitors take to the streets. After yet another year of scratching out a living and surviving the cold of winter, the city unleashes its pent-up inhibitions with a party as wild as Mardi Gras or Carnivale, with a Montana flair. Don't be surprised to see brawling cowboys come tumbling out of any number of imbibing establishments. And unlike in many frontier towns, these fights aren't staged. Another rowdy annual event is **Knievel Days**,

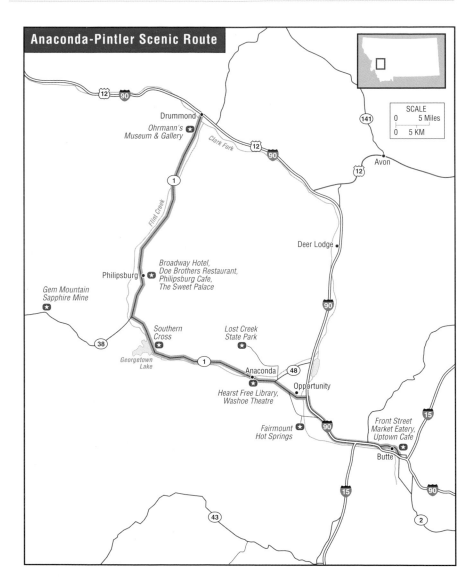

Anaconda-Pintler Scenic Route

named for one of Butte's favorite sons and a magnet for up to 50,000 bikers each July. Both are fueled by ales and brews from the **Quarry Brewery** (406-723-0245), which has plans to relocate in the Grand Hotel and has filled a local handcrafted beer void since 2007.

Just over the hill off I-90, tucked into a gap in the mountains south of the freeway, is the former company town of **Anaconda** (pop. 9,088). It's easily recognized from a distance by the 585-foot smelter stack on the edge of town, the world's largest freestanding structure when built in 1919. The

Stack, as it's known by locals, is now a state park, though not open to visitors. This was where the ore mined in Butte was processed, and with Anaconda Copper's purchase of mines in Mexico and Chile, no smelter in the world produced more copper.

If you've got kids in tow, consider taking a side trip between Butte and Anaconda to the **Fairmont Hot Springs** ($$$, 406-797-3241/800-332-3272), a large hotel and golf complex in the country with two mineral hot pools and two Olympic-sized swimming pools. Don't go expecting peace and quiet, though: Fairmont is full of family activity. Take Exit 211 from I-90, drive about 3 miles to the resort, then go north on County Road 441 to the junction of MT 1 at Opportunity. The hot springs are at the foot of the state-owned, 56,000-acre **Mount Haggin Wildlife Management Area**, the state's largest wildlife area and ideal habitat for pronghorn, white-tailed and mule deer, elk, moose, and an occasional black bear. Another off-the-beaten-byway option worth the 10-mile drive is **Lost Creek State Park** (406-542-5500), featuring 50-foot Lost Creek Falls and 1,200-foot limestone cliffs. The park is known for its mountain goats and bighorn sheep, which endured a lethal pneumonia epidemic in 2010. To get there, turn north on County Road 273 near the junction of MT 1 and MT 48, go left 2 miles later on Forest Service Road 683, and drive about 7 miles.

Anaconda is a long, narrow community, called An-da-CON-ta by residents. Back in the heyday, copper king Marcus Daly built an amusement park here; what's left is the simple **Super Copper Chute** in Charlotte Yeoman Martin Park, a free 140-foot slide the kids might enjoy. The town's fortunes fluctuated wildly with the copper industry, and when the smelter was shut down in 1980, the community was devastated. The weariness still shows, though as cleanup of mining messes forges ahead there are efforts to reinvent Anaconda, à la Butte. The **Old Works Golf Club** (406-563-5989), marked by rusted mining equipment, was designed by Jack Nicklaus and is considered one of the outstanding courses in the country. It was built on the site of a dismantled smelter, and some of the ruins are visible from the course. The stately **Hearst Free Library** (406-563-6932) is another masterful example of century-old architecture. The library was created and then packed with books and art by infamous newspaperman William Randolph Hearst's mother, Phoebe, who developed an abiding affection for Anaconda during visits to Montana. The library has been a community gathering spot since 1898. If you're here in the evening, take in a movie at the ornate **Washoe Theater** (406-563-6161), an art deco palace built in

1931 and once chosen the fifth most beautiful theater in the nation by the Smithsonian Institute.

Anaconda's motto is "Where Main Street Meets the Mountains," and that's just what happens as you head west on the officially designated Anaconda-Pintler Scenic Route. MT 1 weaves upstream along Silver Creek for about 15 miles before reaching Silver Lake, and then goes over a small divide to **Georgetown Lake,** a popular 3,000-acre summer and winter playground squeezed between the Flint Creek and Pintler ranges. Boaters ply these waters, usually in pursuit of landlocked kokanee salmon or football-shaped rainbow trout. The lake has a marina, four boat ramps, three national forest campgrounds, and numerous vacation cabins tucked into the pines. This is a snowmobiler's paradise, and 5 miles to the north is **Discovery Ski Basin** (406-563-2184). The small ski area geared to locals is unique in that the green, blue, and black diamond runs are generally segregated instead of interspersed.

Also on a south-facing hill are remnants of one of numerous ghost towns in the region and the one with perhaps the most extraordinary story: **Southern Cross.** After the mining heyday ended in the 1950s, many families remained. The last of the old-time miners died in 1991, and by then a steady stream of eclectic newcomers arrived, looking to escape mainstream culture. They moved into the old homes scattered across the hillsides, lovingly renovated them, and paid little or no rent to the long-departed Anaconda Mining Company. In effect, they were squatters. When a new company bought the rights to the leases in 1988, they wanted the residents out. Few departed. In the end, Magellan Co. allowed the residents to stay for $150 per year. Today, a mere handful of full-time residents remain, but the handiwork of those who restored the community remains.

From Georgetown Lake's outlet, MT 1 dives precipitously into a canyon carved by Flint Creek as it plunges toward the Philipsburg Valley. A worthwhile side trip after emerging from the canyon is a drive up MT 38 to the **Gem Mountain Sapphire Mine** (406-859-6463/866-459-4367) about 12 miles west of the junction. For about $15 a bucket, you can wash gravel over a trough while looking for sapphires—with a certainty you'll find at least a dozen small gems and perhaps even land a whopper. The mine is usually open Memorial Day Weekend through September, weather permitting.

Back in the valley, the highlight of the Anaconda-Pintler journey unquestionably is the old sapphire, ruby, and corundum mining community of **Philipsburg**—or, once you've mingled with the 900-plus friendly locals for a few hours, simply "P-Burg." The town was built on the side of a hill and enjoyed boom times in the late 1800s. Today, it has been colorfully restored. Scanning Broadway Avenue, you'll quickly understand why Philipsburg has twice been a finalist for "Prettiest Painted Place in America."

It's easy to spend an entire day wandering the streets of P-Burg, given the plethora of shops related to the town's history. The aforementioned **Gem Mountain** is one of three purveyors of the uniquely clear and colorful sapphires, discovered in Rock Creek in 1892. Other places to shop for loose stones and/or finished jewelry: **Opal Mountain Gems** (406-560-7469) and **The Sapphire Gallery** (800-525-0169), which will evaluate other stones or gems you own. And for a genuine step back in time, the **Granite Ghost Town State Park** (406-542-5500, May–Sept.) 4 miles outside Philipsburg offers walking tours of what's left of a community built around the richest silver mine in the world.

Leaving Philipsburg, MT 1 heads north along Flint Creek into a broad valley of ranches and Angus cattle. The one-blip communities of Maxville and Hall have some history worth taking a peek at, but save time for a visit to the **Ohrmann Museum & Gallery** (406-288-3319), which is less than 3 miles south of Drummond. The gallery and yard-art menagerie features 92-year-old proprietor Bill Ohrmann's one-of-a-kind works (see sidebar). If it's after hours, just pull into the driveway, and Ohrmann or his wife will soon

Life-sized sculptures in Bill Ohrmann's yard lead you to the oil paintings inside his gallery.

emerge from the house to open the gallery. The route ends where Flint Creek meets the Clark Fork and MT 1 meets I-90. Drummond has a close-knit populace with the usual handful of taverns, gas stations, and cafés, but the main attraction takes place on Friday nights in the fall when the powerhouse Trojans football team plays.

If your tour takes you back to Butte on I-90, stop at Deer Lodge to visit the **Grant-Kohrs Ranch National Historic Site** (406-846-2070), once the hub of a 1-million-acre cattle operation and now 1,600 acres of trails, artifacts, historic buildings, museum collections, and other interesting remnants from Montana's open-range era. The self-sustaining ranch features all of its original livestock breeds and still uses old-time equipment. Operated by the National Park Service, the ranch is open daily except Thanksgiving, Christmas Day, and New Year's Day and is less than 2 miles from I-90 on the north end of Deer Lodge.

Best Places to Bunk

Butte: For less than a king's ransom, you can sleep at the appropriately appointed **Copper King Mansion** ($$, 406-782-7580). Run by the brother and sister team of John Thompson and Karen Sigl, the three-room Victorian built for U.S. Senator William A. Clark was (and continues to be) a fixer-upper when their grandmother bought it in 1953. Even if you're not staying, take a tour and find out the secrets of the copper czar. **Toad Hall Manor** ($$/$$$, 406-494-2625), a B&B in a five-story brick mansion, is a world made better with its tea and scones. Toad and Mole would have thought they'd died and gone to the high willows for a sleepover and breakfast at the Manor.

Anaconda: The **Hickory House Inn** ($$, 406-563-5481) on East Park Avenue downtown is a five-bedroom B&B created from what was the rectory of St. Paul's Church. The bright and cheerful colors include the outdoor gardens and thematic rooms, and the gourmet breakfast is a cut above.

Philipsburg: The historic nine-room **Broadway Hotel** ($$/$$$, 406-859-8000) is P-Burg's best-known lodging; a continental breakfast is included. **The Kaiser House** ($$, 406-859-2004) has been a favored gift shop, but now the upstairs has four rooms authentically renovated for lodging. Each room is dedicated to pertinent history, and the mural room painted by local artist Liz Silliman is a tribute to local color. Just off Broadway Avenue is the **McDonald Opera House** ($, 406-859-0013), a 350-seat classic western stage with comedy and vaudeville performances June through

Labor Day. During the off-season, between Labor Day and Memorial Day, you can bunk in one of eight cobweb-free rooms—no charge for the occasional ghost that reputedly has been recorded saying "hello." If you're looking for out-of-the-norm, try the **Biker's Sanctuary** ($/$$, 406-859-1003), where the Grateful Dead meets the Holy Grail in a converted old church readily visible up the hill east of downtown. Owners Dave and Kim Chappel spent years traveling astride motorcycles and kept notes about what amenities were lacking for their type of road warrior. A well-polished "hog" takes center stage among a pulpit, pew, and pipe organ in the entry to a parlor painted ornately by the ubiquitous Silliman.

Alternative Bunking

Camping: Lost Creek State Park (406-542-5500) is a frequently full spot with 25 primitive first-come, first-served sites and no fee. The Beaverhead-Deerlodge National Forest has eight campgrounds along the Pintler Scenic Route. Coming from Anaconda, 14-site Spring Hill campground is on the right just past the junction of FS 170 and Warm Springs Creek, about 2 miles before Silver Lake. Georgetown Lake has three Forest Service campgrounds: **Piney** (47 sites), **Lodgepole** (30 sites), and the popular **Philipsburg Bay** (67 sites). Piney and Philipsburg Bay have lakeside sites, while Lodgepole is across MT 1 from the lake. If you like ATVs and dirt bikes, the **Cable** campground above the lake on Forest Service Road 65 is for you; the 11 sites offer instant access to old logging and mining roads. For those who prefer to stretch out streamside, **Flint Creek** campground offers 16 spots at the bottom of the precipitous descent on MT 1, including two walk-in sites for tenters.

Forest Service Cabins/Lookouts: (Reservations: 877-444-6777 or www.recreation.gov.) The Butte and Pintler ranger districts offer many primitive cabins for nightly rental, including four close to the route: They are **High Rye Cabin** ($20/sleeps four), **Douglas Creek Cabin** ($20/sleeps six), **Moose Lake Guard Station** ($20/sleeps four), and **Stony Cabin** ($20/sleeps four). High Rye is in a retired mining area called German Gulch and popular with the motorized set. Douglas Creek, about 10 miles northwest of Philipsburg, is accessible by car for much of the year. Moose Lake Guard Station, about 25 miles southwest of P-Burg, also can be reached by car virtually year-round. Stony Cabin is favored by anglers pursuing trout in Rock Creek.

Best Eats

Butte: For quieter moments, sit down to a civilized artful meal and wine list at the **Uptown Cafe** ($$, 406-723-4735, L [weekdays]/D), where the cuisine rivals big-city dining. In a hurry? Grab some homemade goodness to-go from Jim and Marla's Italian-style **Front Street Market & Deli** ($, 406-782-2614, L). The place is packed from floor to ceiling with specialty foods and is a great place to pick up wine or unique beer.

Anaconda: **Classic Cafe** ($/$$, 406-563-5558, B [weekends]/L/D) has family fun painted all over its white-and-black checkered exterior and a friendly menu of pizzas, salads, and wraps (brace yourself for the super-spicy habanera chicken wrap). Dinner highlights include hand-battered fresh halibut with chips, calzones, and pasta plates. Check out the authentic Herbie the Love Bug and his girlfriend Millie in the dining room.

Philipsburg: You can't go wrong at **The Philipsburg Cafe** ($$/$$$, 406-859-7799, B/L [Wed.–Sun.]/D [Fri.–Sat.]), where owner/chef Mike Sauer, an immigrant from Boston and a Red Sox fanatic, has found a way to meld upper-crust East Coast tastes with a laid-back local preference. Stepping into **Doe Brothers Soda Fountain and Restaurant** ($$/$$$, 406-859-7677, L/D) is like entering a way-back machine to the 1920s, but with a modern menu. Popular lunch items include the black-and-blue burger and Jiminy Cricket chicken salad sandwich, while a trio of buffalo, elk, and beef medallions and maple, pepper buffalo flank steak headline the dinner selections. The soda fountain dishes up such local Wilcoxson's ice cream favs as huckleberry, buffalo chip, and A Chocolate Runs Through It. You can put on five pounds just browsing in **The Sweet Palace** (406-859-3353), a sweet-tooth magnet for its staggering assortment of fudge, saltwater taffy, truffles, and caramels, most made on-site. And if you can't find your favorite jelly bean here, it simply doesn't exist.

Best Bar

Anaconda: For a snapshot of what club life was like in the 1930s, look no farther than **Club Moderne** (406-563-7593) on East Park Avenue. The club does more than wink at an era of suit coats, fedoras, pink ladies, and sidecars. One look at the neon exterior sign, curved building, and rounded door window explains why it's listed on the National Historic Registry.

OHRMANN MUSEUM AND GALLERY: ONE FOR THE AGES

Just before he unlocks the door to his deceptively modest gallery just south of Drummond, Bill Ohrmann leans on a hand-carved wood cane and pauses. "It's not for everybody," the lean, 92-year-old former rancher cautions, peering out from under a cowboy hat.

"OK to think your own thoughts" reads the last of four lines of large type on a hand-painted sign at the entrance, just above small type that adds: "Crackpot tho they might be."

Ohrmann flips a switch, illuminating a backroom chock-full of smaller sculptures and colorful oil paintings covering nearly every inch of wall space, all gorgeously framed and lighted. One after another reveals his fondness for the earth, its creatures, and long-ago cultures that knew how to live harmoniously with both—along with a harsh indictment of his own culture and the roots of its rapacious attitude toward the land. He leaves no traditional Montana avocation untouched: logging, mining, grazing, hunting, motorized recreation, and, above all, doing it in the name of God.

Ohrmann didn't begin painting until he was 78, when he retired from ranching and handed the reins to his children. His first gallery showing came after his 80th birthday. Some of his paintings speak for themselves; for others, he uses quotations from renowned poets and conservationists. His best-selling print shows a content man and his dog, accompanied by a quote from Abraham Lincoln: "I don't think much of a man's religion if it makes no difference how he treats his dog."

Another painting was born from a story his father told him more than 80 years ago of a soldier he'd known who fought against the Nez Perce in the bloody 1877 Battle of the Big Hole not far from the family ranch. "How Colonels Become Generals" is the caption accompanying an image of a soldier gazing proudly upon burning teepees—the devil at his side.

The Ohrmann Museum & Gallery, on the west side of MT 1, is easy to spot. The yard around the gallery is filled with unusual welded-metal sculptures, most notably an 11-foot-high mastodon.

Step inside to the long backroom to find red, tuck-and-roll vinyl seats, speckled Formica-topped tables, and wood inlay all integral to the Streamline Moderne style. Skinny Francesco opened the club in 1937, and it was the swingingest place for miles. The black-and-white photos on the walls will dial you back to a time of snappy Sinatra songs, highballs, polished shoes, and bouffant 'dos. Owned by John and Stephanie Hekkel since 1999, it's now an any-age bar—a place to relax, watch a game, throw some darts, or chat up the bartender.

The Perfect Weekend

Start your Friday night by checking into the **Copper King Mansion** and then visit a few of the museums in Butte the next morning. Have lunch at the **Front Street Market Eatery & Deli**, and then at Anaconda peek inside the **Washoe Theater**, browse the **Hearst Free Library**, and have a beverage at **Club Moderne** before heading into the mountains. At **Georgetown Lake**, veer off the main road for a brief driving tour of the old **Southern Cross** mining town while enjoying views of the lake. Arrive midafternoon in **Philipsburg** and check into the **Broadway Hotel** for the night. After freshening up, take a walking tour of P-Burg and take out something for dessert at the **The Sweet Palace** before having dinner at the **Doe Brothers Soda Fountain and Restaurant.** Rise early for a hearty breakfast at **Philipsburg Cafe** and then backtrack to **Gem Mountain Sapphire Mine** in hopes of striking the mother lode—or at least nabbing one gleaming sapphire. Head down the Flint Creek Valley, where you'll want to take in the **Ohrmann Museum & Gallery** en route to Drummond and consider an oil painting for a one-of-a-kind souvenir (see sidebar). Head back to Butte for a microbrew at Quarry and experience some of the state's finest dining at the **Uptown Cafe.**

DETOUR: ONE FOR THE ROAD

The Skalkaho Highway

Porters Corner to Hamilton

Estimated length: 71 miles

Highlights: Skalkaho Pass, Sapphire Mountains, Gem Mountain Sapphire Mine, Rock Creek, Skalkaho Game Preserve, Skalkaho Falls, Daly Mansion.

Getting there: Exit I-90 either at Anaconda (Exit 208) or Drummond (Exit 163) to reach the highway from the east side; each approach is on MT 1, the Anaconda-Pintler Scenic Route. From the west, take US 93 at Missoula and head south through the Bitterroot Valley to Grantsdale, about 3 miles south

Skalkaho Falls between Philipsburg and Hamilton is a highlight of the drive.
Donna Mitchell

of Hamilton. For an extra adventurous approach—especially if you're a fly angler—take the Rock Creek turnoff on I-90 (Exit 126) and drive south along the creek, one of Montana's blue-ribbon trout streams, to the road's meeting with MT 38 about 12 miles west of Porters Corner.

Don't be fooled by the state-highway designation. For at least one-third of its length, MT 38 between the Flint Creek and Bitterroot valleys is anything but a highway. It's a narrow, twisting gravel road through some of southwest Montana's prettiest scenery.

Skalkaho comes from the Salish words *skalen* (beaver) and *kalalko* (green woods), the literal translation being "beavers of the green woods" and the direct reference being to Skalkaho Creek. For generations, the Salish used this route over the Sapphire Range, and then in 1924, the state and Forest Service built the current road to facilitate access to the mines. The highlight—literally and figuratively—is 7,260-foot **Skalkaho Pass** at the crest of the north–south Sapphires, so-named for their abundant minerals. This drive is purely about scenery and wildlife viewing; there are no services or any other commercial endeavors except for the **Gem Mountain Sapphire Mine** about 13 miles into the route along **Rock Creek**. The road rises gently to the pass from the east side along the East Fork Rock Creek, through a variety of forest lands, then descends more noticeably on the west to the Bitterroot Valley.

Porters Corner is at the junction of MT 1 and MT 38, about 6 miles south of Philipsburg. As you turn west on MT 38, look for moose in the willows on Flint Creek. In about 9 miles the paved road reaches East Fork Rock Creek, the headwaters of one of western Montana's premier trout fishing destinations. The upper stretches get less pressure because of the distance from Missoula, so there's a good chance you'll have the creek to yourself.

After following East Fork Rock Creek for about 5 miles, the West Fork joins to form the main branch of Rock Creek. The "highway" follows the West Fork Rock Creek on paved road for about 4 miles before turning into a glorified Forest Service Road that's closed for all but summer and early fall to automobile traffic (the groomed trails are popular among snowmobilers). A few miles before reaching the summit is the primitive **Crystal Creek Campground**, with three sites. At the pass, FS 1352 veers to the north toward the **Skalkaho Game Preserve**, a 23,000-acre forest and meadow area known for its birds, elk, deer, and occasional black bear. Three twisting miles below the pass is the route's primary attraction: the oft-photographed **Skalkaho Falls**, a popular day-hiking and picnicking area. The falls tumble 150 feet over rocks just off the road.

From the falls, the road bends to the southwest and follows Daly Creek to a Darby Ranger District station and **Black Bear Campground**, another primitive Forest Service site with six camp spots. **Hamilton** (pop. 3,705), where the notorious Calamity Jane once operated a café, was a timber town now recasting itself as a tourist destination. Attractions include the **Daly Mansion**, built by former copper magnate and town founder Marcus Daly, and Rocky Mountain Laboratories, which was created to combat Rocky Mountain spotted fever but has since evolved to study some of the world's most dangerous diseases.

Beaverslide haystackers are the symbol of the Big Hole Valley, and are still in use on many area ranches.

The Land of 10,000 Haystacks: The Big Hole Valley and Pioneer Mountains Scenic Byway

Dillon to Polaris

Estimated length: 113 miles
Estimated time: 6 hours to 2 days

Highlights: Beaverhead River, Bannack State Park, Jackson Hot Springs, Big Hole National Battlefield, Big Hole River, Pioneer Mountains, Elkhorn Hot Springs, Maverick Mountain Ski Area.

Getting there: From I-90, there are two ways to come at this diverse loop—both involving I-15. Start at the Divide exit on I-15 and cut through the Big Hole River Canyon on MT 43 to Wise River, where the loop begins either with an immediate left turn onto the Pioneer Mountains Scenic Byway or by continuing west along the Big Hole River toward Wisdom.

Another approach is to start and finish in Dillon. Take Exit 59 three miles south of Dillon and drive west, following the signs for Bannack State Park and Wisdom. In about 20 miles, you'll have to decide whether to continue straight toward Jackson and do a clockwise loop, or veer right and follow Grasshopper Creek to go counterclockwise between the East and West Pioneers. We suggest going clockwise.

Overview

Even in the heart of summer, watching silver-tipped clouds race just overhead is enough to make a knowing Montanan shiver. The Big Hole Valley is

Cattle, haystackers, and mountainous backdrops are common fixtures on the Pioneer Mountains Scenic Byway.

known for extreme cold—cold air, cold water, and bone-chilling history. The air in this high mountain valley in the far southwest corner of the state is so crisp and dry that hay is safely stored in the open, stacked by the stately wood-plank beaverslide haystackers that look like giant catapults from medieval days. The water is so brisk that the sparkling Big Hole River is home to a native population of fluvial Arctic grayling, a revered native fish making its last river stand in the Lower 48 here. And speaking of last stands: You can't help but feel a bit melancholy upon visiting the haunting Big Hole National Battlefield, where the peace-loving Nez Perce's gallant pursuit of freedom in 1877 suffered an irreparable blow in this high mountain valley.

This is the Big Hole country, a remote and rugged region spreading out below the backbone of the Rocky Mountains. The Lewis and Clark expedition explored this country in 1805 on its journey west—and then years returned over Gibbons Pass west of present-day Wisdom. In fact, William Clark himself came up with the name "Wisdom," a nod to President Thomas Jefferson's foresight. The river's name was changed to the Big Hole before the 19th century was out, but Wisdom lives on in a tiny community that looks much like a setting for a shoot-'em-up western.

The symbol of the "Land of 10,000 Haystacks" is the beaverslide, invented and patented in the valley in 1910 and a staple today even as other regions evolve to more modern technology and smaller stacks. These giant wooden contraptions are responsible for the prolific large stacks of hay throughout the valley. Though many haystackers in the Big Hole are now made of metal, the technique is the same: Horses or tractors use belts to ease the hay up the slide and then flip it over into a roll the size of a small barn. For a time it appeared the beaverslide would go the way of the passenger pigeon, but it's undergoing a revival as high fuel costs have ranchers looking for more economical ways to preserve a lifestyle.

Hitting the Road

We suggest starting and finishing the Land of 10,000 Haystacks/Pioneer Mountains Scenic Byway loop in **Dillon** (pop. 3,752), where you'll find all the necessary services. Dillon is a longtime ranching, logging, and mining town grudgingly evolving to a place where aesthetics, wildlife, quiet recreation, and intrinsic values reign. The upgrade of its four-year school, Montana-Western, from a teachers' college to a full-fledged university, along with a gradual influx of newcomers, is changing the culture. That said, the town is in no immediate danger of becoming a Bozeman, Missoula, or Whitefish even though the environs are as beautiful, rugged, and appealing.

Dillon has several worthwhile stops. The **Beaverhead County Museum** (406-683-5027, Mon.–Fri.), in a log building along the railroad downtown, offers an array of pioneer artifacts, including the city's first flush outhouse toilet, a homesteaders' cabin, mammoth bones, and plenty of old mining and logging equipment. A mile northeast of town on MT 41, **Clark's Lookout State Park** (406-834-3413) is on a bluff overlooking the Beaverhead River where Captain William Clark, separated from a fretting Meriwether Lewis and his party, climbed on August 13, 1805, to survey the valley. The pair reconnected three days later at a site now submerged in Clark Canyon Reservoir south of Dillon.

To get to the loop, leave I-15 three miles south of Dillon at Exit 59 and head west on MT 278. After traveling through sage and grass ranchlands

A must-see on the route for pure tourist aesthetic pleasure is **Conover's Trading Post** (406-689-3272, May–Nov.), which was a hotel until a 1960 fire caused havoc in Wisdom. Although owner Judy Mohr is divorced from Mr. Conover, she kept the name for the sporting goods/souvenir/snack stop's national recognition. Part of the Conover allure: the reclining "Indian lady" covering most of the building's classic western front. She is adorned with jewelry, but given her ample physical attributes no one seems to notice.

The brisk Big Hole River begins to gather some volume at Wisdom and becomes one of the state's most revered trout streams as it moves north. What makes this stretch truly one-of-a-kind is the opportunity to catch six—count 'em—varieties of fish: the imported rainbow trout, brook trout, and brown trout as well as the native whitefish, cutthroat trout, and Arctic grayling. Farther downstream, the river is famed for its early summer salmon-fly hatch and early fall caddis hatch, both of which lure fly anglers from the world over.

For the next 30 miles, MT 43 hugs the river and, after passing Country Road 569 to Anaconda, veers east into a pine-studded canyon with trophy homes and summer getaways. Eleven picturesque miles later, the Big Hole emerges into a modest valley at **Wise River** (pop. 128). This is a great place to pick up a few necessities at the **Wise River Mercantile** (406-832-3271) and find out what the trout are rising to at the **Complete Fly Fisher** (866-832-3175). Just before the Wise River Club, look for an unmarked right turn on FS 484—here begins the **Pioneer Mountains Scenic Byway** portion of the route. The 49-mile north–south road, now fully paved, rises gently toward the headwaters of the Wise River and descends through the heart of the mountains along Grasshopper Creek, splitting the towering and rugged East Pioneers from the gentler West Pioneers. This section has numerous campgrounds and trails north of the divide, including the federally designated **Pioneer Loop National Recreation Trail** (406-832-3178) near the upper reaches of the Wise River, **Browns Lake Trail** just before the divide, and the **Blue Creek Trail** near Elkhorn Hot Springs farther south. The 35-mile **Pioneer Loop Trail** isn't for the faint of heart, but this strenuous hike along the backbone of the West Pioneers provides dramatic vistas of the Big Hole Valley; it's reached from the main road by turning right on FS 90 about 20 miles south of Wise River. Browns Lake Trail is near the junction of FS 2465, which leads to **Coolidge** ghost town. Drive about 5 miles to the trailhead and hike another quarter mile to the abandoned

Long, lonely stretches of highway characterize touring the Grasshopper Valley.

Elkhorn Mine and town, which is remarkably well preserved due largely to its isolation.

Atop the gentle divide, the road levels and provides regular views of the rugged East Pioneers, which some compare to the Swiss Alps. There are several scenic turnouts, most notably **Mono Park** and **Moose Park**, where interpretive signs explain why the East Pioneers are so different than the West Pioneers. The **Lupine Picnic Area** has a small warming hut amid lodgepole pines that's amply stocked with firewood. Also near here is **Crystal Park** (406-683-3900), a day-use area where the Butte Mineral & Gem Club and Forest Service provide a summer opportunity to dig for quartz crystals. The 30-acre site has water, picnic tables, and trails to the digging sites, which look a little like minefields. A $5 fee is charged, but you may keep any crystals you find.

Over the divide and in the tall timber, accommodations at **Elkhorn Hot Springs** (406-834-3434) are as primitive as Forest Service cabins, but the pool is a delightful respite of gravity-flow, sulfur-free warm water. Many of Elkhorn's visitors spend their day at **Maverick Mountain Ski Area** (406-834-3454), an intimate and out-of-the-way ski hill with 22 runs and 2,000 vertical feet. At $30 for a lift ticket, you can get your money's worth "Riding the White Thunder" on a credible variety of terrain.

Polaris (pop. 107), named by miners for the polar star, has a fitting moniker for this area: It's a popular location for snowmobiles. From Polaris, it's another 6 miles back to MT 278 and the end of your loop. Look for a few more of the beaverslide haystackers that epitomize this region. Turn left on MT 278 for the drive back over Badger Pass to Dillon.

"I SHALL FIGHT NO MORE FOREVER"

Of all the Indian tribes encountered by settlers of the frontier, none earned more respect and admiration than the Nez Perce of Idaho, eastern Oregon and Washington, and western Montana. They helped Lewis and Clark cross the Bitterroot Range during a bitter winter, perhaps saving the expedition. They were as receptive to the white man's ways as any tribe. Many became Christians and changed their names to reflect their conversion.

Yet their cooperative and peaceful ways didn't prevent the Nez Perce from suffering the same indignant fate as the rest of their brethren in the late 1800s—banishment to reservations on a fraction of their ancestral lands.

For the Nez Perce, life amid their natural riches ended in 1877 after a remarkable three-month pursuit that covered five states and 1,170 miles. Many Nez Perce had already signed a treaty requiring the tribe to move to a small reservation in northern Idaho, but a handful of "nontreaty" members led by chiefs Joseph, Whitebird, and Looking Glass refused to leave much larger homelands that were ceded to them in a previous treaty.

Ordered to move his people and livestock to the Idaho reservation, Joseph instead began a march eastward, hoping to find sanctuary with the Crows in south-central Montana—unaware that the tribe had aligned with the cavalry and had fought with Custer at Little Bighorn. For weeks, Joseph and his 700-plus Nez Perce—two-thirds women and children—outwitted General O. O. Howard and his 2,000 soldiers; they even handed the army a defeat at White Bird Canyon above Idaho's Salmon River in mid-June, shortly after leaving the sacred Wallowa country of northeastern Oregon.

After crisscrossing the Bitterroots between Idaho and Montana, the turning point came on August 9 at the Battle of the Big Hole west of present-day Wisdom. Until then, the Nez Perce had the upper hand in their skirmishes even as they fled, but the loss of 25 warriors at the Battle of the Big Hole left them on the defensive. They crossed five-year-old Yellowstone National Park, where they killed two tourists, and ascended the Absaroka Mountains into the Clarks Fork of the Yellowstone River Valley. Once back into Montana southwest of Billings, they discovered the Crows wouldn't help them because they feared retribution.

From there, the Nez Perce charted a course due north, hoping to find a new home in Canada with Sitting Bull and a band of Sioux. They fell 40 miles short. It was at the Bear's Paw Mountains, his tribe freezing and starving, that Chief Joseph uttered his famous surrender speech on October 6, 1877: "Hear me, my chiefs! I am tired; my heart is sick and sad. From where the sun now stands I will fight no more forever."

Today, the route the Nez Perce took is the federally designated Nee-Me-Poo Trail. It was added to the National Trails System in 1986.

Best Places to Bunk

Dillon: The town has a handful of comfortable chain motels and a few small independents but unique options are limited. Best bet is probably the **GuestHouse Inn & Suites** ($$, 406-683-3636). You'll surely notice the century-old **Metlen Hotel & Saloon**, which once offered a slice of Dillon history but is on the market; even the saloon was no longer open as of September 2010. Built in 1897 along the Union Pacific tracks, the Metlen is the only remaining stately hotel from Dillon's prosperous railroad and extractive-industry days,

Jackson: Jackson Hot Springs Lodge's ($/$$, 406-834-3151) cabins and motel aren't for everyone. The sleeping rooms are just that, barely big enough for a bed, and you can hear your neighbors think. The larger rooms with fireplaces are on the musty side. But as of December 2010, the place was under new ownership, so perhaps brighter days are ahead for this stopover with tons of potential.

Wisdom: The **Wisdom Cabin** ($, 406-689-3800), a gathering place for women during World War I, is today a light, bright, cheery one-bedroom place where up to four guests can hang their rod or skis. The cabin has a remodeled interior and original log exterior. Owners Diane and Dennis Havig offer a stay-and-ski package for $50 per night.

Polaris: Lodging is sparse on this section of the loop. You'll find 10 primitive cabins—some remodeled, none with running water or inside toilets—and 10 basic rooms with shared baths at **Elkhorn Hot Springs** ($/$$, 406-834-3434). A small breakfast and admission to the hot springs pool are included. The **Grasshopper Inn** ($, 406-834-3456) is basic, but the attached restaurant and saloon (B/L/D) serve up surprisingly good eats and family-friendly hospitality daily during the high season; hours vary the remainder of the year. South of Polaris, the **High Country Guest Lodge** ($$, 406-834-3469) is a classic hunting lodge with 12 rooms overlooking a pond in the Grasshopper Valley, with expansive views of the Pioneers. Though walk-ins are welcome for dining and guests can choose the number of days they stay, a minimum four-night stay is required for fishing, winter sports, and cattle-drive packages, and it's six nights for hunting packages.

Alternative Bunking

Dillon: The 57-acre **Beaverhead Rock Ranch** ($$, 406-683-2126) offers both an original two-bedroom farmhouse and a one-bedroom, authentic log cabin at the mouth of a canyon on the Beaverhead River for rent— two nights minimum. The renovated cabin was a cook house moved log by log from another ranch and rebuilt on its present site not far from the river. Gary Williams's spread is next to 350 acres of leased Bureau of Land Management ground, which includes a huge beaver-shaped rock cliff rising straight from the river.

Wise River: The **Big Hole River Cabins** ($$$/406-832-3271) are sweet and rustic and offer private access to great fishing on the Big Hole two miles outside town. Each of the two cabins sleeps four and has all the basic amenities for a self-sustained stay.

Camping: The **Dillon KOA** (800-562-2751) on the town's west side is quiet and well kept and offers a secluded area for tenters along the Beaverhead River, which has fine trout fishing. The KOA has 30 sites for tents, 68 for RVs, and wireless Internet. There are five small first-come, first-served primitive Forest Service campgrounds on paved loops along

Front-yard fishing and privacy are the trademarks of the cabin on the Beaverhead Rock Ranch near Dillon.

the Pioneer portion of the loop. Our favorites are **Lodgepole** and **Willow**, both sheltered in the pines on the banks of the Wise River. The **Mono Campground** is up a gravel road near the Coolidge ghost town and has five tent sites.

Forest Service Cabins/Lookouts: (Reservations: 877-444-6777 or www.recreation.gov.) The **Birch Creek Cabin** (406-683-3900, $20/sleeps four) requires driving about 12 miles north of Dillon on I-15 and turning west at Apex for another 8 miles into the mountains, but it's the only Beaverhead-Deerlodge National Forest offering of its kind in the Pioneers. The primitive cabin is isolated enough from the ubiquitous motor crowd that it's popular with hikers and cross-country skiers looking to explore the range's high lakes.

Best Eats

Dillon: **Sparky's Garage** ($/$$, 406-683-2828, B/L/D), next to the University of Montana-Western, is like a scene from the *Route 66* TV show, with the signage and décor to match; consider the barbecue brisket, chili, and cornbread, or the catfish basket. For the best steak and fine-dining ambience in town, it's the **Blacktail Station** ($$, 406-683-6611, D). The western-themed restaurant is in an old mine shaft below **Mac's Last Cast** bar and boasts more than a substantial steak (smothered sirloin heaped with grilled onions), seafood (Alaskan king crab legs), and pasta (house-made lasagna) with four entrée-qualifying salads—go for the Blacktail with blue cheese, dried cranberries, sunflower seeds, bacon, and more.

Jackson: **Jackson Hot Springs** ($$/$$$, 406-834-3151, B/L [Sat.–Sun.]/D [daily]) has received its share of plaudits and has a welcoming river-rock fireplace in the main lodge. The dining room is unique in that the seafood is as good as its steaks; the garlic-crusted prawns are a favorite.

Wisdom: The palate-pleasing **Crossing Bar & Grill at Fetty's** ($/$$, 406-689-3260, B/L/D) added gourmet touches to western-style comfort food—heavy on the breading (mushrooms, dill pickles, shrimp) and meat (certified angus and bison)—and is renowned for its jams and jellies. Now in its new location, Big Hole Crossing kept a few of the Fetty's favorites, including the pioneer burger and super nachos.

Wise River: Like many Montana saloons, the **Wise River Club** (406-832-3258) is best known for its burgers, especially the double-pattied hamburger steaks, each weighing 6 to 8 ounces. Slapped together, they might require two people to reel it in, especially when served with their tasty hand-cut french fries.

Best Bar

Wise River: Among a string of interesting bars along the Big Hole River between Wise River and Divide, the **Wise River Club** (406-832-3258) stands out in part because it's the most inviting for nonlocals. This is the place to belly up and learn what the trout are hitting from local outfitters, who arrive soon after the last cast to chug a concoction called the "guide's drink"—vodka, Cock 'N Bull ginger beer, and lime served in a copper mug. The club is divided between a small café and large bar. On the bar's ceiling are the impressive antlers of a single bull elk that lived a prosperous life for more than two decades in a corral across the highway, augmenting his ample rack each year. After an evening of pool or shuffleboard, you can retire upstairs to one of six spartan rooms—each with one bed (communal bath and shower down the hall) for $65 a night. Out back are two cabins with two queen beds, bath and shower for $85 a night.

Wise River Club serves up lodging, good eats, and an adult-beverage concoction called the "guide's drink."

The Perfect Weekend

Arrive in Dillon to check into the **GuestHouse Inn & Suites** and have dinner at the **Blacktail Station**. Start the morning with eggs and bacon at **Sparky's Garage** and then spend the morning wandering amid the remarkably preserved buildings of the ghost town at **Bannack State Park**, southwest of Dillon. Stop and snap a few photos of beaverslide haystackers before arriving in Jackson for a soak at **Jackson Hot Springs**. In the afternoon, set out for the **Big Hole National Battlefield** and listen for the echoes as you wander amid the pines. Back in Wisdom, check into the **Wisdom Cabin** and have dinner at the **Crossing Bar & Grill at Fetty's**. In the morning, stop at **Conover's** to stock up on flies before heading out for a morning of casting to rising trout on the Big Hole River. Arrive in Wise River in time for lunch and a "guide's drink" at the **Wise River Club** and ice cream from the **Wise River Mercantile**. Spend the afternoon driving the Pioneer Mountain National Scenic Byway, saving time to explore the **Coolidge** ghost town and dig for quartz crystals at **Crystal Park**. Have a home-style dinner at the **Grasshopper Inn** before returning to Dillon.

DETOUR: ONE FOR THE ROAD

The Bitterroot Valley

Missoula to Lost Trail Pass

Estimated length: 95 miles

Highlights: Historical Museum at Fort Missoula, Elk Country Visitor Center, Lee Metcalf National Wildlife Refuge, St. Mary's Mission, Fort Owen, Lake Como, Lost Trail Pass, Lost Trail Hot Springs Resort, Lost Trail Powder Mountain.

Getting there: Leave I-90 either on US 12 in downtown Missoula (Exit 105) or US 93 (Exit 101, Reserve Street) and head south along the Bitterroot River.

Long before outsiders discovered the aesthetic wonders of the Flathead and Whitefish, the Bitterroot Valley became synonymous with the Montana mystique. Though Missoula author William Kittredge's famous "Last Best Place" description was actually coined in a trailer house in the Paradise Valley, he drew much of his inspiration from the Bitterroot.

The Bitterroot is an exceptionally pretty north–south valley known for its moderate climate, prolific trout fishing, and high quality of life. One old timber town after another—Missoula, Lolo, Florence, Stevensville, Victor, Hamilton, Darby, and Conner—has become a bastion of 20-acre ranchettes and a jumping-off point for outdoor adventures in the wild Bitterroot Mountains.

At the north end of this route is progressive **Missoula** (pop. 64,081). Fueling the town's energy is the University of Montana, which has churned out conservation activists to rival any East or West Coast university. Think Berkeley and Madison, with hiking boots, skis, and fly rods. Missoula still has a raw side reminiscent of the town's old Front Street honky-tonks, an image that only adds to an intrigue that has been tempered by the relatively recent arrival of strip malls, big-box stores, and traffic.

Missoula has enough diversions to fill several days, but if time is short be sure to hike the switchback **Mount M Sentinel Trail** to the "M" above the university. The Rocky Mountain Elk Foundation's 22-acre **Elk Country Visitor Center** features terrific dioramas of elk in their natural environment and an outdoor hiking trail. The organization is largely responsible for restoring elk populations depleted by wanton hunting at the turn of the previous century. For an interesting look at Missoula's frontier history, the **Historical Museum at Fort Missoula** on the southwest edge of town looks at the area's military history, including exhibits about the Buffalo Soldiers bicycle corps—a group of black men who pedaled from Missoula to St. Louis, Missouri, as part of a U.S. Army experiment to see if bicycles could replace horses as the cavalry's primary mode of transportation.

Nine miles south of Missoula, after US 93/12 slips through a neck between the Bitterroot and Sapphire mountains, US 12 splits to the west at **Lolo** (pop. 4,887) and begins a 31-mile ascent to Lolo Pass and Idaho. This was Lewis and Clark's most famous crossing of the Rockies.

US 93 follows the Bitterroot past a series of river access points and through a procession of inviting communities, starting with the one-time sawmill town of **Florence** (pop. 901)—formerly called One Horse, for the creek that arrives in town from the flanks of the Bitterroots. Between Florence and Stevensville is the **Lee Metcalf National Wildlife Refuge**, named after a Montana senator from the Bitterroot who would become one of the state's great conservation champions. The watery refuge, created in 1963 as a safe stopover for migratory birds, has more than 2 miles of hiking trails and a gravel road that offers excellent waterfowl viewing.

Stevensville (pop. 1,967) was actually Montana's first Anglo community, begun as **St. Mary's Mission** in 1841 by the Jesuit priest Pierre DeSmet. The mission chapel has been restored and is a museum that features furniture belonging to the pioneering priest Anthony Ravalli, who built it. Nine years after DeSmet's arrival, Major John Owen built the trading and military post on the site he would call **Fort Owen**. The state's first gristmill, sawmill, and school for settlers was here. What remains is a barracks housing artifacts from Owen's day, plus some reconstructed buildings.

Next up on the road south is **Victor** (pop. 859), once a silver mining community. Named after a Flathead chief, Victor was the site of the lucrative Curlew Mine. The area's mining, timber, and railroad history is captured well in the **Victor Heritage Museum**, located in the old Northern Pacific depot.

South of Victor is **Hamilton** (pop. 3,705), after which the valley begins to narrow and takes on more of the characteristics of the "old Montana." Ranchettes and subdivisions, though creeping south, give way to a rural and ranching persona. Just past Como Bridge, Lake Como Road follows Little Rock Creek for about 3 miles to Lake Como, which was raised for irrigation purposes to be a full-fledged reservoir and features a Forest Service campground with 10 RV sites. This is the only handicapped-accessible equestrian campground in the western United States, revealing the popularity of pack trips into the Selway-Bitterroot Wilderness Area straddling the Montana-Idaho border.

Three miles south of Como Bridge is cozy and resilient **Darby** (pop. 710). Three times Main Street burned, and three times the town bounced back. Darby has ridden an economic rollercoaster: first fur trading, then mining, timber, apples, and ranching. As each has waned, tourism and the accompanying shops have become a staple, and Darby is a popular base for pack trips and whitewater excursions into the Selway-Bitterroot.

Continuing south, the east and west forks of the Bitterroot join just north of the little logging wayside of **Conner** (pop. 250), which has three restaurants and a small motel. After Conner, US 93 begins its ascent along the East Fork Bitterroot River through woodsy **Sula** (pop. 10) toward **Lost Trail Pass** on the Montana-Idaho border. Four miles east of Sula on the East Fork Road is the **Broad Axe Lodge & Restaurant**, which features two rustic cabins and fine dining and is designated by the state as a wildlife-viewing area for its prolific number of critters. Back on US 93, the **Lost**

Trail Hot Springs Resort at Sula has cabins, two lodges, and an RV park and is a great place to soak in the natural waters of the hot tub or swimming pool after a day on the runs at **Lost Trail Powder Mountain** ski area, a family-oriented operation open Thursday through Sunday from December until April.

Latigo & Lace in Augusta has a little bit of everything Montana, including books and classy gifts as well as a cappuccino bar.

CHAPTER

6

On the Edge of Wilderness: The Rocky Mountain Front

Wolf Creek to Browning

Estimated length: 136 miles
Estimated time: 6 hours to 2 days

Highlights: Milford Colony, Sun River Game Preserve, Old Trail Museum, Pine Butte Swamp Preserve, Teton Pass Ski Area, Miller Colony, Two Medicine Dinosaur Center, Egg Mountain, Museum of the Plains Indian, Scapegoat and Bob Marshall wilderness areas.

Getting there: From I-90, go north on I-15 out of Butte through Helena to the US 287 exit 2 miles north of Wolf Creek. This is what Lewis and Clark referred to as The Gates of Mountains. Upon leaving the freeway, you'll cross a strip of the Rocky Mountain Front onto the prairie.

Overview

The Rocky Mountain Front technically stretches from the Canadian border near Glacier National Park to northern New Mexico, but for the most part only here can you see the great American prairie as it once was—sweeping, undulating, largely unscarred native rangelands rising gently to meet the sheer walls of the Northern Rockies and the rugged Bob Marshall Wilderness, known simply to locals as "the Bob." This is classic A. B. Guthrie country, the famed author of westerns who lived outside Choteau.

The country is so rare and striking that it stirred a rare coalition of locals—ranchers, Blackfeet, business owners, recreationists, politicians, and even energy companies—to protect the Front from drilling and subdivision, retaining its ruggedness for current and future generations. By the summer of 2010, the Rocky Mountain Front Heritage Act was moving closer to fruition in Congress, ensuring that a roughly 100-mile strip from East Glacier south to Rogers Pass will enjoy unique blend of protections: wilderness, a special conservation zone, and efforts to help family ranchers remain on the land.

The movement began in 1977 when a Pendroy taxidermist and Choteau elementary schoolteacher started Friends of the Front, with the support of ranchers and sportsmen who saw the looming energy development ending a way of life—much the way it already had in parts of New Mexico and Colorado. Their concerns were heard by Lewis and Clark National Forest supervisor Gloria Flora, who had the rare courage to ban oil and gas drilling on the Front at a time when her brethren were rubber-stamping leases across the West.

Because of the three-decades-long efforts, and because of the care that multigenerational cattle-ranching families have had for an unforgiving landscape where Chinook winds come howling off the mountainsides at up to 100 mph, people are living, working, and playing in harmony with nature here. And you get to immerse yourself in a rare world.

The Front is home to the second-longest elk migration in the United States. Grizzlies wander the foothills and plains. In June 2010, two bears sauntered more than 100 miles across the plains to the Missouri River between Great Falls and Fort Benton, the first time in a century that the great bear has been to the edge of the Missouri Breaks.

The Rocky Mountain Front byway starts in ponderosa pines near the Gates of the Mountains at Wolf Creek and ends in rolling sage country just east of Glacier National Park in Browning, site of the Blackfeet tribal headquarters. Along the way you'll pass through the charming ranching communities of Augusta, Choteau, and Dupuyer; while Choteau is A. B. Guthrie's home, Dupuyer is the setting for many Ivan Doig works. It'll take some discipline to resist the urge to gaze out the driver's side of the car toward the jagged Wailing and Castle Reefs, especially at sunrise and sunset.

Lodging and dining are available, but consider staying in Helena before you start. Take a tour of the state capital—its decor captures the essence of

Montana as well as any building in the state, and you just might see the governor, wearing blue jeans and a bolo tie, wandering the hallowed halls with his dog.

Hitting the Road

As you come north from Helena on I-15, you're on what was once a toll road through a pine canyon between Fort Benton and Helena. Today, **Wolf Creek** (pop. 735) at Exit 226 is a jumping-off point for fishing on the trout-rich Missouri River and Holter Lake.

The route begins 2 miles later at US 287 (Exit 228). The highway immediately begins a gradual rise out of the pines through the Front, denoted by undulating grass prairie, piney ridges, coulees, and periodic rivers, starting with the Dearborn. Amid grazing cattle, look for mule deer and pronghorn—the second-fastest land mammal in the world—in the 27 miles between I-15 and the junction of MT 200 at Bowmans Corners. Just to say you've been there, take a brief detour about 20 miles west on MT 200 to 5,610-foot **Rogers Pass**, which registered the coldest temperature ever in the Lower 48: minus-70 degrees on January 20, 1954. If you're there in the spring or fall, you might witness the extraordinary migration of nearly 1,000 golden eagles between the mountains and plains. Many people are drawn to this spectacle on a 1,300-acre area near the pass, where the predators ride the thermals seemingly within an arm's reach.

To the west now are such limestone peaks as Blowout, Table, Steamboat, and Lone Chief, which rise from the **Scapegoat Wilderness Area**. Just past Bowmans Corners is the 12,000-acre **Milford Colony**, one of about 40 Hutterite communities across Montana. The Hutterites—or

The Hutterites sell their produce, poultry, and baked goods in nearby communities.

"Hoots," as they are commonly called—are a self-sufficient, independent, and peaceful people of eastern European descent who live simple agricultural lives similar to the Amish and Mennonites. Colonists frequently ven-

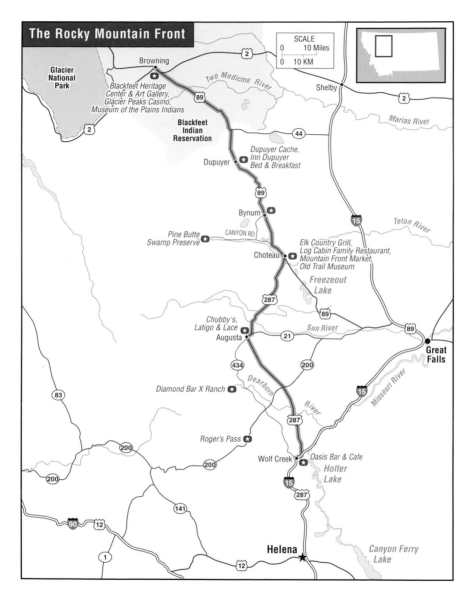

The Rocky Mountain Front

SCALE
0   10 Miles
0   10 KM

Glacier
National
Park

Browning

Blackfeet Heritage
Center & Art Gallery,
Glacier Peaks Casino,
Museum of the Plains Indians

Two Medicine River

Shelby

Marias River

Blackfeet
Indian
Reservation

Dupuyer Cache,
Inn Dupuyer
Bed & Breakfast

Dupuyer

Bynum

Pine Butte
Swamp Preserve

CANYON RD

Teton River

Choteau

Elk Country Grill,
Log Cabin Family Restaurant,
Mountain Front Market,
Old Trail Museum

Freezeout
Lake

Chubby's,
Latigo & Lace

Augusta

Sun River

Great
Falls

Diamond Bar X Ranch

Dearborn

River

Missouri River

Roger's Pass

Wolf Creek

Oasis Bar & Cafe

Holter
Lake

Helena

Canyon Ferry
Lake

ture out to sell baked goods, produce, turkeys, chickens, and crafts in rural communities. Stop by for fresh vegetables and fryers.

For the next 75 miles, wildlife, history, and western personalities are the name of the game. **Augusta** (pop. 785) is a sweet little cottonwood oasis near the Sun River, with great views of the Rockies. **Latigo & Lace** (406-562-3665, Mar.–Dec.) is a made-in-Montana gem with fine arts, pottery, photography, a wide array of books, an espresso bar, and a great deal more.

Near Gibson, west of Augusta, is the **Mortimer Gulch National Recreation Trail**, a moderately challenging serpentine trek that features grassland views. This area is a popular starting point for hikers wanting to cross the Bob Marshall Wilderness Area and reach the sheer Chinese Wall, "the Bob's" signature geologic feature. Tucked inside the wilderness is the **Sun River Game Preserve**, created in 1913 as elk summer range to salvage what was left of herds devastated by the arrival of the white man. Thirty-four years later, with elk thriving, the **Sun River Game Range & Wildlife Management Area** was created on the Front Range for wintering elk and is one of the finest places in Montana to see the herds. And if domestic four-legged critters are your thing, the popular **Augusta American Legion Rodeo** in late June is Montana's oldest.

Back on US 287, the highway eases away from the Front Range, but the views remain spectacular. About 25 miles northeast is **Choteau** (pop. 1,781), which justifiably dubs itself "The Front Porch of the Rockies." Choteau is a comfortable town that's ideal for an overnight to explore the heart of this region. Before leaving Choteau, visit the **Old Trail Museum** (406-466-5332, May–Sept.), a collection of frontier buildings that house artifacts from eras ranging from a century ago to millions of years. The museum, so-named because it's on the 25,000-year-old Old North Trail once used by the ancestors of the Blackfeet, is part of the state's dinosaur trail. It also has an exhibit featuring Guthrie, the first great western writer born and raised in Montana. Perhaps the most memorable display is of an old French trapper standing upright despite having an arrowhead lodged in his spine.

In Choteau, veer north on US 89. If you're a bird aficionado, take an hour-plus detour southeast about 12 miles the other direction on US 89 to **Freezeout Lake**, a key spot on a migratory flyway for prolific flocks of waterfowl. Back in Choteau, you'll have a decision to make: Continue northwest on US 89 about 9 miles, then drive about 5 miles to the junction of Canyon Road, which follows the Teton River west past Eureka Reservoir and opens up the Front to a wide variety of recreation opportunities. Be sure not to miss The Nature Conservancy's 15,500-acre **Pine Butte Swamp Preserve** (406-443-8311, see sidebar), a vast and stunning plains wetlands complex at the edge of the mountains. For an extraordinary weeklong experience, you could arrange an all-inclusive stay at the conservancy's **Pine Butte Guest Ranch** ($$$$, 406-466-2158, May–Sept.) and take part in nature courses, workshops, and conservation-related activities in stunning landscapes.

Continuing up Canyon Road, there are no fewer than three designated hiking trails epitomizing the diverse terrain: **Mill Falls Trail** is an easy hike through thick forest, **Clary Coulee Trail** represents the rolling prairie landscape, and **Green Gulch Trail** combines both with a nice dose of mountains. For winter enthusiasts, picturesque **Teton Pass Ski Area** (406-466-2209) is a small family ski area with two lifts (no lines), 26 runs, and 1,010 feet of vertical drop.

As you return toward US 89, you can continue straight to the highway and visit the **Hutterite Miller Colony.** Another option is to go left about 10 miles before US 89 at the Bynum Reservoir turnoff and reconnect with the main highway at **Bynum** (pop. 77), a diminutive town with a giant dinosaur—in fact, the world's largest. The **Two Medicine Dinosaur Center** (406-469-2211) is home to the skeletal display of a *Seismosaurus* and also features the remains of the first baby dinosaur found in North America; the museum has regular summer hours and requires an appointment the rest of the year. While you're there, ask about joining a dig at **Egg Mountain**, an excavated area beneath a rise on US 89 just south of Bynum, where you might run into famed paleontologist Jack Horner. Fossilized eggs were found in Maiasaura nests in 1983, and dinosaur remnants are regularly found. Across the street from the museum in Bynum is the seeing-is-believing **Trex Agate Shop** (406-469-2314). John Brandvold's selection and collection of rocks, gems, and artifacts is updated annually and rivals anyone's in the world. It was his wife, Marion, who reportedly found the first nest of baby dinosaurs at Egg Mountain in 1978—five years before the paleontologists. Her life is quite a story, and well worth a sit-and-chat if you catch John with some free time. Like the museum, the shop has regular summer hours and is open by appointment at all other times.

Angling northwest of Bynum, the highway continues its undulating course toward **Dupuyer** (pop. 181), an endearing one-blink town along Dupuyer Creek. For goodies, the quaint **Dupuyer Cache** (406-472-3272, 11 AM–5 PM, Wed.–Sat.) combines many of the amenities of an old mercantile, from groceries and dry goods to local honey, crafts, and wool that comes from one of those old-school beaverslide haystackers in the Big Hole Valley.

A few miles outside Dupuyer is the southern boundary to the 3,000-square-mile **Blackfeet Indian Reservation**, home to about 8,500 tribal members. The once-powerful Blackfeet, frequently referred to as "The Lords of the Great Plains," believe they were created on these lands about 6,000 years ago. The Montana Blackfeet (called Blackfoot in Canada) call

Bynum's Two Medicine Dinosaur Center has the world's largest dinosaur skeleton.

themselves Piegans or Pikanni. Among Indians, they have the unique distinction of retaining their most sacred lands, though it's largely because Anglos had little use for the blustery high plains.

US 89 crosses nearly 40 miles of foothills country, dipping and rising in and out of creek and river bottoms, before arriving in the Blackfeet capital of **Browning** (pop. 1,079). Feeling as if they'd entered a foreign country, tourists have often clenched their steering wheels a little tighter passing through Browning en route to Glacier or Alberta's Waterton Lakes National Park. But as the Blackfeet undergo a cultural rebirth of sorts, they are making Browning more hospitable. Where the Rocky Mountain Front drive ends, with US 89 meeting US 2, is the **Museum of the Plains Indian** (406-338-2230, admission in summers/free Oct.–May)—a must for anyone who appreciates the rich history of native peoples. No fewer than 11 Plains Indian tribes are represented here. The museum is under the auspices of the Indian Arts and Crafts Board, so you know you'll be getting authentic

THE FRONT: WHERE THE MIGHTY GRIZ ROAMS THE PRAIRIE

Once upon a time, the mighty grizzly bear, king of the wilderness food chain, roamed the Great Plains by the tens of thousands. But by the late 1800s, westward Anglo expansion and a determined effort at extirpation pushed the great bear into small mountain nooks, mostly in Greater Yellowstone and the Crown of the Continent ecosystems.

A notable exception is the Pine Butte Swamp Preserve, where the grizzly has continued its annual spring migrations from the expansive Bob Marshall Wilderness Area to the prairie. In 1979, The Nature Conservancy purchased these 15,500 acres of foothills and prairie and a 500-foot sandstone butte solely to provide a lowland outlet for the grizzly, which arrives via the Teton River corridor.

Grizzlies have made a solid comeback in the Northern Rockies in the past three decades, though they remain under Endangered Species Act protections because of the disappearance of some of their primary food sources—especially the high-elevation whitebark pine, which is dying at prodigious rates. Except for the Pine Butte Swamp Preserve and a small slice of the Blackfeet Indian Reservation to the north, though, they have not been tolerated on the prairies.

Our willingness to live with these majestic and fearsome creatures is being tested. With grizzly numbers expanding in wilderness areas and national parks, more are wandering onto the prairies in search of new space. In the summer of 2010, several wandered through the preserve, past Choteau, and all the way to the Missouri River—about 100 miles. Montana wildlife officials trapped the bears and took them back home. Grizzlies are occasionally seen in creek bottoms all along the Front.

Expectations are that grizzlies will continue to move to lower elevations in search of food, raising fears of increased confrontations between humans and bears. When that happens, bears usually die.

At Pine Butte, the mindset is different. It's the bear's world, and humankind is to tread lightly. Spend a week in the summer or just a weekend in the spring or fall, and marvel at the idea that somewhere deep in one of those green creek bottoms is a grizzly contentedly living the way its ancestors did a century ago.

stories in words and pictures. The **Blackfeet Heritage Center & Art Gallery** (406-338-5661, Mon.–Sat. summers) is another place to get a poignant understanding of native culture. The center sells Indian jewelry, moccasins, beadwork, baskets, drums, and other items. A memorable time to be in Browning is the second week of July for **Northern American Indian Days,** a four-day powwow where colorful teepees seem to extend to the horizon.

For fishermen, the Blackfeet Reservation is a paradise of lakes, rivers, and streams. Believing waters hold mystical powers, the Blackfeet traditionally haven't fished, and so there are dozens of small lakes and potholes, eight large lakes, and nearly 200 miles of streams filled with big trout and other species; stop in Browning for a tribal permit. Browning does have a few motels and restaurants, but the most appealing options are in East Glacier—about 15 miles west but still on the reservation.

Best Places to Bunk

Augusta: The nine-room **Bunkhouse Inn** ($, 406-562-3387) is a basic old-west-style hotel in a century-old structure that has retained its flavor. Two shared bathrooms are at the end of the hall, and the porches on either end of the building are a place to catch some fresh air. The **Diamond Bar X Ranch** (406-562-3325, May–Oct.) offers nine guest cabins, full horse accommodations, and a campground with RV hookups in the Dearborn River canyon south of Augusta.

Choteau: The **Stage Stop Inn** ($$/$$$, 406-466-5900) is appealing to families because of its indoor pool and Jacuzzi—the only heated indoor pool within 50 miles, they like to say—and amenities like continental breakfast and kennels for hunting dogs. You can also find a little luxury and room to spread out in their king suites. The 14-room **Bella Vista Motel** ($, 406-466-5711) is a clean stop well suited to a couple and a throwback to the motor-court era.

Dupuyer: The town's size makes the rural **Inn Dupuyer Bed & Breakfast** ($$, 406-472-3241), with its three single rooms and two-bedroom suite in a log home, feel like a real getaway—complete with a full breakfast and sensational mountain views. The inn is in a century-old home that has been restored and renovated; all five rooms have baths.

Alternative Bunking

Choteau: The **Choteau RV Park Campground** (406-466-2615) features three cabins, 49 RV sites, 20 tent sites, and running water—no showers—in a relatively urban setting by rural Montana standards.

Forest Service: A plethora of Forest Service campgrounds are located on the Lewis and Clark National Forest west of Augusta and Choteau. **Home Gulch** (15 sites) and **Wood Lake** (9 sites) campgrounds are 20 and 24 miles west of Augusta, both peaceful places on a lake where motorboats are prohibited. Two miles beyond Wood Lake is **Mortimer Gulch** (28 sites), which has a boat launch and is the largest of the Rocky Mountain Front campgrounds. Another 4 and 5 miles up the road are **Benchmark** (25 sites) and **South Fork** (7 sites) campgrounds, both popular jumping-off points for Bob Marshall Wilderness forays. Another four campgrounds are northwest of Choteau: **Cave Mountain** (14 sites), **Elko** (3 sites), **Mill Falls** (4 sites), and **West Fork** (6 sites). Elko and Mill Falls are free, and the other two offer quick access to "the Bob."

Best Eats

Wolf Creek: Save your appetite for **Oasis Bar & Cafe** ($$, 406-235-9992, B/L/D), on the east side of the freeway in Wolf Creek. The café specializes in made-to-order food, including hand-pressed burgers, creative soups, and its most expensive dinner entrée: an extra-large New York steak with all the trimmings for $24. Also at the café is Alva Lee Baking, a bakery serving pastries, tea, and coffee from 6 to 11 AM, seven days a week. In the dead of winter, you can have your meals in the bar, when the café side is closed.

Augusta: Across the street from Latigo & Lace, **Chubby's** ($, 406-562-3408, B/L/D)—formerly Mel's Diner—has typical fare but is best known for its ice cream and pie; Chubby's serves dinner, but only until 7 PM. For more robust ambience and meals as well as great service—often from Ginger, who's been taking care of her customers for 28 years—there's the **Buckhorn Bar** ($/$$, 406-562-3344, L/D, see Best Bars). The **Lazy B Bar & Cafe** ($, 406-562-3550, L/D) in an 1883 building is where most days you'll find a dinner special, fresh-cut meats, and homemade pizzas.

Choteau: John Henry's ($, 406-466-5642, B/L/D [Wed.–Mon.], B [Tues.]) offers large portions of classic Montana fare for modest prices. The **Elk Country Grill** ($$/$$$, 406-466-3311, L/D) is the favored spot to have a sizzling steak, elk medallions, or walleye accompanied by home-made soup, a bottle of red wine, and a slice of pineapple upside-down cake or fresh-baked pie for a filling finish. For lunch, give the Indian taco

Start your Rocky Mountain Front journey with a home-cooked meal at the Oasis Bar & Cafe in Wolf Creek.

a whirl. The **Log Cabin Family Restaurant** ($$, 406-466-2888, B/L/D) has excellent bison burgers, a walleye dinner that will bring you back for more, and between 20 and 25 home-baked pie choices. But, it might be best known for its most famous patron: late-night talk-show host David Letterman, who has a ranch nearby, frequently eats there. Choteau is also hip enough to have a health-food store—the **Mountain Front Market** (406-466-2684, 11 AM–6 PM, Mon.–Sat.)—stocked with all the requisite healthy food and drink for a long hike into the Front country or for cooking your own meals.

Browning: There isn't much to choose from in the capital of the Blackfeet Nation, but at the **Glacier Peaks Casino** they want to keep you happy so the food at the **Jackpot Restaurant** ($, 406-338-2274, B/L/D) is reasonable and decent. Specials include a brunch buffet from 11 AM to 2 PM on Sundays and prime rib on Friday nights.

Best Bar

Augusta: Montana bars and taxidermy are synonymous, but the classic western **Buckhorn Bar** ($/$$, 406-562-3344, B/L/D) in Augusta takes animal wall mounts to another level. There are dozens of racks on the log beams overhead as you chow down on their claim-to-fame broasted chicken (Grandma Dellwo's secret spice blend is in the coating) and handmade Montana beef burgers. All menu items are less than $10 except for the 16-ounce rib steak with baked potato and salad for just under $18. The Buckhorn opens at 8 AM and closes at 2 AM, making it one of the few good choices in the area for early or late eats; after 11 PM, you'll have to settle for a pizza. The Buckhorn has been in the Dellwo family for four decades and is a regional icon. Before it burned to the ground in 1974, the kitchen was in a trailer off to the side. Now the Buckhorn is in an attractive and intimate log building, complete with a photo on the wall of Grandpa Dellwo's smiling face. He seems to be saying: "Life is all good in Montana."

The Perfect Weekend

Get your weekend started right with a supersized New York steak or almost-gourmet cooking at the **Oasis Bar & Cafe** in Wolf Point. Heading northwest, grab a hearty western breakfast of bacon, eggs, and pancakes at **Chubby's** in Augusta. You'll want to get your caffeine and shopping fix at **Latigo & Lace**, where you'll have a visual feast of western art, books, and jewelry. After Augusta, plan to spend some time in the Choteau area, starting with a visit to the western-themed **Old Trail Museum**, and then swing into the **Log Cabin Family Restaurant** for a bison burger or walleye, a side of fries, and a slice of heaven in the form of several pie flavors. Choteau is a great place to leave the route and explore the foothills to the west; before heading for the hills, pick up some healthy snacks at the **Mountain Front Market**. Up the road are three options for stretching the legs and getting some exercise. Choose from the diverse **Mill Falls, Clary Coulee**, and **Green Gulch** trails. Pick the one that best suits your interests and fitness level. Back on US 89, wander around the **Two Medicine Dinosaur Center**

Get your health-food fix for the road at the Mountain Front Market in Choteau.

and **Trex Agate Shop** across the highway from each other in Bynum. Even if John's gem shop is closed, give him a call, and he'll happily open up. Though it's backtracking, return to Choteau for a Montana-style dinner at the **Elk Country Grill** before heading north to Dupuyer for a night at the **Inn Dupuyer Bed & Breakfast**. After breakfast at the inn and a stop at the **Dupuyer Cache** for some local goods (after 11 AM), look for the serrated peaks of the Bob Marshall Wilderness and Glacier National Park off to the west. Upon arriving at the Blackfeet tribal headquarters at Browning, sandwich tours of the **Museum of the Plains Indian** and **Blackfeet Heritage Center & Art Gallery** around lunch at the **Jackpot Restaurant** in **Glacier Peaks Casino**.

Detour: One for the Road

The Kings Hill Scenic Byway
White Sulphur Springs to Belt

Estimated length: 71 miles

Highlights: Spa Hot Springs Motel, Showdown Ski Area, Neihart, Monarch, Sluice Boxes State Park.

Getting there: Exit I-90 just east of Livingston at US 89 and drive north through Clyde Park, Wilsall, and Ringling—of Ringling Brothers Circus fame—until reaching White Sulphur Springs.

Sometimes "scenic byway" isn't always about the scenery. Case in point: the Kings Hill Scenic Byway. Oh, there is plenty of classic Montana landscape to see. The distant Crazy, Bridger, and Absaroka mountain ranges ring the skyline, looking like so many sets of bad teeth.

Nevertheless, when the U.S. Forest Service—which owns a fair chunk of the real estate on this route—deemed the 71 miles between White Sulphur Springs and Belt one of its "scenic byways," it had an ulterior motive. The Forest Service motto is "Land of Many Uses," and few drives in Montana display the state's three-pronged utilitarian history more than this one. The majority of the drive is through the modest Little Belt Mountains, an isolated 1,800-square-mile range that rises to more than 9,000 feet and is the first Rocky Mountains visitors see coming from the east on US 12. Surrounding the Little Belts is ranchlands with Angus cattle as far as the eye can see. Scattered throughout the pine- and fir-covered range is extensive evidence of their grazing, logging, and mining history. It is, in many senses, a snapshot of Montana, captured in two to three hours.

The Forest Service wants you to understand and, hopefully, appreciate an extractive legacy that is waning in favor of recreational and aesthetic values on public lands. Kiosks at both ends of the route describe the hum of industry that once echoed across the hillsides. Distant checkerboard hilltops with young stands of lodgepole pine surrounded by mature trees reveal a timber industry gone silent. Rusted and splintered remnants of mining operations are visible from the road at once-booming Neihart. Cattle and periodic gas wells show that the utilitarian age isn't completely over.

Even the recreation here tends toward the motorized: snowmobiles in the winter, all-terrain vehicles in the summer.

That said, don't be dissuaded by the lack of jaw-dropping vistas. There is plenty of charm here. In addition, if you're national-park hopping between Yellowstone and Glacier, this is both the most direct and most intriguing route. It offers the healing waters of the **Spa Hot Springs Motel** at White Sulphur Springs, where you can soak away the aches of a hard day and then literally enjoy pizza and a movie at the same time at **Stageline Pizza**. At Kings Hill Pass, it also features **Showdown**, the oldest continually operating ski area in Montana. Heading down the north side, **Neihart** and **Monarch** are the living remnants of the area's mining days. As you emerge from the mountains, the **Sluice Boxes State Park** offers a peek into mining history and, when the water levels are right, a thrilling whitewater ride reminiscent of the log flumes at amusement parks.

At the end of the route is the little community of Belt, which has recovered from the demise of the coal-mining industry and a devastating train derailment in 1976 to become a charming evening getaway for residents of Great Falls. The **Harvest Moon Brewing Company** in Belt is admired regionally for the microbrews offered in its tasting room and elsewhere, most notably the Beltian White. For dinner on the weekends, try the **Black Diamond Bar & Supper Club** and its surprisingly gourmand menu, or the **Black Creek Brew Pub**.

Libby has a proud, but checkered, mining and logging history.

CHAPTER

7

Forests and Free Spirits: The Yaak River Country

Libby/Rexford/Yaak/Troy

Estimated length: 175 miles
Estimated time: 5 hours to 2 days

Highlights: Forest-fire lookouts, Kootenai Falls, Libby Dam, Lake Koocanusa, Yaak River Falls, Turner Mountain Ski Area.

Getting there: Take the St. Regis exit from I-90 and double back on MT 135 to a meeting with MT 200. At the junction of MT 200, go west and keep following the Clark Fork through Paradise and Plains to Thompson Falls—a great place for a meal or snack break. Continue northwest through Belknap, Whitepine, and Noxon to MT 56. Turn north toward Troy and Libby, passing the turnoff for the towering conifers at Ross Creek Giant Cedars Nature Trail. From there, it's 20 miles to US 2 and the beginning of Yaak River Country.

Overview

Whatever accessories are on a checklist for your travels through the Yaak River Country, be sure it includes a book by the valley's most famous resident: author Rick Bass. The most obvious is *The Book of Yaak,* but our favorite is *Winter: Notes from Montana,* about spending a long winter amid the mist, curling woodstove smoke, and eclectic folks in the state's most mystery-enshrouded corner.

Bass's insights explain the Yaak's fundamental appeal, which stems not just from its literal and figurative distance from anywhere but also from what its thick forests and foggy mountaintops leave to the imagination. Though other parts of Montana are more remote and have fewer people, most feature the wide-open spaces and distant snowcapped mountains for which the state is famous. Secrets are easier to keep in the Yaak. Along the Yaak River Road, narrow two-track driveways disappear into the shadows, leaving passersby and even delivery folks to guess what lurks amid the darkness of lodgepole pine, western larch, and Douglas fir forests. In some cases FedEx drivers are simply instructed to leave packages "on the orange X."

Electricity didn't arrive here until 1963—other than the lights powered by a grumpy diesel generator at the Yaak's once-notorious Dirty Shame Saloon—and many families still live "off the grid," without electricity or plumbing, along this spectacularly scenic river. The stream gets its start in British Columbia as the Yahk River, exchanges the *h* for a second *a* as it crosses into the United States, and begins a swift, often-frothy 45-mile southward journey toward a meeting with the brawny Kootenai River below US 2. The Yaak's serpentine path suggests anything but its name—Kootenai for "arrow." At its midpoint, the river passes through the valley's largest community, Yaak, where some of the valley's 500 or so aging hippies, loggers, and Forest Service employees emerge from the woods and close the day at the Dirty Shame—or used to, anyway. The newest owners have scrubbed the layers of grit from the saloon and made it downright family friendly.

The mellowing of the Dirty Shame and Yaak Mercantile across the road epitomizes the evolution of this country. Where once the forest was abuzz with the whine of chain saws and the thunder of logging trucks, now an environmental ethic has taken root, championed by the likes of Bass and others who are trying to preserve the last vestiges of America's vanishing old-growth forests. Remnants of the old logging days are still visible, but today such towns as Troy, Eureka, and Libby are more oriented to outdoor recreation and visitors who come to hike a remote mountain trail, hunt a trophy bull elk, or photograph an elusive wolf slipping in and out of the shadows.

The Yaak River Country route traverses a gravel mountain pass, traces either shore of the caterpillar-shaped Lake Koocanusa (KOOtenai River, CANada and USA) and includes the relatively populated US 2—the country's northernmost coast-to-coast highway.

Hitting the Road

Assuming your journey starts at the junction of US 2 and MT 56 just outside Troy, head east toward Libby first. Within 5 miles is the most awe-inducing natural wonder on the loop: **Kootenai Falls**. The Kootenai River funnels through a rocky gorge that the Kootenai worshiped as the center of their universe. Other great waterfalls of the Pacific Northwest have been inundated by dams, but today visitors are transfixed by the spectacle of 50,000 cubic feet of water per second thundering through the S-shaped canyon. Take a walk over the swinging bridge just downstream from the cascading whitewater, too. If the falls look familiar, this is where guide Meryl Streep used her river guile to outwit the evil Kevin Bacon in the 1993 movie *The River Wild.*

For a longer hike with more exertion, stop another 6 miles past the Kootenai Falls parking area at the **Scenery Mountain Lookout Trail**. Turn right on Cedar Creek Road and drive 3 miles to the trailhead. The last half of the 5-mile hike is on the arduous side, but the views looking south from the lookout into the Cabinet Wilderness are impressive.

Back on US 2, it's a few more miles into **Libby** (pop. 2,921), a deceptively attractive town of 3,000 with a checkered history. A quarter century after a company called W. R. Grace began mining vermiculite, a Seattle newspaper ran a series investigating an extraordinary number of deaths due to related asbestos contamination. The town is still reeling (see sidebar). Don't let this legacy stop you from spending a few days here, though; Libby could use a morale and economic boost. Besides, its people are cheerful, the Cabinet Mountains backdrop is dramatic, and the fishing on the broad Kootenai River between the town and Libby Dam about 17 miles upstream is as exceptional as it is intimidating. The state-record rainbow trout, a whopping 33-inch football weighing 38 pounds, was caught just below the dam, and Montana's largest native whitefish, a 5-pounder, was landed in the same stretch. Check out the **Heritage Museum** (406-293-7521, summers), which captures the area's rich mining, logging, railroading, and American Indian history, among other topics.

The first stop after leaving Libby on MT 37 is the massive **Libby Dam** and its informative visitors center (406-293-5577, summers). At 422 feet high and 3,055 feet long, the dam creates **Lake Koocanusa**, a caterpillar-shaped body of water that backs up for 90 miles, pushing 40 miles into British Columbia. The structure, completed in 1972, was built to tame the

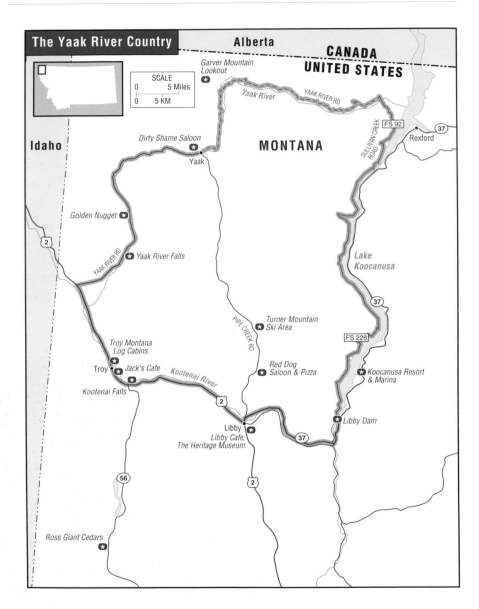

mighty Kootenai's spring flooding and also provide hydropower. Guided tours are available in the summer.

From Libby Dam, there are two choices for continuing the journey northward along Lake Koocanusa, between the Salish and Purcell mountains. MT 37 hugs the eastern shore, and the less-traveled FS 228 winds through pines on the west side. Both are paved and equally scenic; if you're not in a rush, take FS 228. In winter, there is no choice—FS 228 is closed once the snows fly. To find lodging and dining, take MT 37. Five miles north of the dam is **Koocanusa Resort & Marina** (406-293-7474, Apr.–Dec.), which offers cabins, 81 RV sites, camping, a restaurant, and a small general store. The resort is best known for its annual Salmon & Trout Derby, which pits anglers in a competition to land the biggest kokanee salmon and rainbow trout.

About 45 miles north of Libby, a bridge crosses the lake. If you're needing a break, continue for about 6 miles on MT 37 into **Rexford** (pop. 150), which was once on the banks of the Kootenai River but was moved 2 miles to its current location in 1974 after rising lake waters flooded the original town site.

Once back down to the bridge, your navigational skills will be tested. Cross the lake and turn right on Sullivan Creek Road—also FS 92—and follow the shoreline about 3 miles before veering west and beginning an ascent into the wild Yaak River country. A well-maintained gravel road

Lake Koocanusa, which stretches into Canada, is known for its boating and fishing.

climbs over a modest pass, where it remains FS 92 and also becomes the Yaak River Road. As you descend, you'll meet the tumbling waters of the Yaak from the right. At this point, you're less than 4 air miles from the Canadian border, and you might even come across a border patrol agent in a telltale white truck with green markings. When the road bends south, FS 276 juts off to the west toward **Garver Mountain Lookout**, one of the four towers available for rent. If you're into roughing it a bit, these are unforgettable experiences.

After following the Yaak through private lands, look on the right for a pioneer cemetery amid the pines. Headstones dating to the late 1800s poke from a carpet of pine needles and are scattered widely around an American flag pole. The gravel road continues past an occasional private residence to the junction at **Yaak** (pop. 150), home to the **Yaak Mercantile** (406-295-5159), the Yaak-O-Mat Laundromat, and the **Dirty Shame** (406-295-5439), now open year-round. The mercantile's back deck serves up magnificent views of the river through the firs; a nearby trail leads to trout fishing that remains solid despite decades of logging.

Heading south on the Yaak River Road, the first cascade of **Yaak River Falls** is easily seen from the highway and is quite photogenic. More interesting is the lower drop, where water slides down a flat slab of rock at about a 30-degree angle. Some of the exposed rock here is 1.5 billion years old. Also visible are the remnants of a mining bridge. Built in the 1880s as a route to the now-defunct mining town of Sylvanite, it was the first bridge across the Yaak.

Troy's location in the mountains belies its elevation.

After winding through the woods past many of those mysterious gravel two-track driveways, the Yaak River Road ends at US 2. Turn east to **Troy** (pop. 957), where the signs boast "Lowest in Elevation, Highest in Recreation." Set amid the pines and firs, Troy is the last Montana town before the Idaho state line on the Kootenai River, which collects a goodly portion of western Montana's waters. At a decidedly un-Montana-like 1,880 feet above sea level, Troy has relatively mild, albeit damp, winters.

At Troy, the loop is complete. For a bonus adventure, return to Libby, cross the river on MT 37, and make a quick left on Pipe Creek Road—a forested shortcut back to Yaak. Though much of this route is deep woods, and the road gets narrower as it rises over a small divide into the valley of the South Fork of the Yaak, there are three reasons to drive this way: the scenery, **Red Dog Saloon & Pizza**, and **Turner Mountain Ski Area** (406-293-2468). Turner Mountain's lone lift provides access to 25 varied runs, with a 2,110-foot vertical drop from a summit elevation of

Libby's Red Dog Saloon is a peanut-shells-on-the-floor joint with big-screen TV.

5,952 feet. It isn't Whistler, Sun Valley, or even Bozeman's Bridger Bowl, but Turner is among the most remote ski areas in America, so crowds are light. And at $30 for a full-day lift ticket, it's also light on your wallet.

Best Places to Bunk

Libby: Libby has two small motels and two bed and breakfasts, including **Moose Ridge Lodge Bed & Breakfast** ($$/$$$, 406-293-3960)—which is actually two cabins and a lodge room tucked into the woods just off US 2 about 14 miles southeast of town.

Yaak: The Dirty Shame's **Yaak River Cabins** ($, 406-295-5439/406-658-0417) feature six one-room cabins for $35, a little more in the winter to offset propane heating costs. The owners have plans to add electric heat, allowing them to be open year-round, but call to make sure. Speaking of phones, there is no cell service up here, so Gloria allows guests free long-distance calls from her phone in the bar as well as checking e-mail from her laptop. For more upscale accommodations, the hunting- and fishing-oriented **Yaak River Lodge** ($$, 406-295-5463) is an always-busy place down the road. The main lodge has five inviting suites, a communal flophouse with bunk beds on two floors ($40 a person), and a private fishing cabin open only in the summer that sleeps six for $30. Located on the river, its rates include a full sit-down breakfast.

Troy: **Troy Montana Log Cabins** ($/$$, 406-295-5810), on a slight perch just above the west end of town, has four clean and comfortable cabins. **Swanson Lodge** ($$, 406-295-4555), 7 miles southeast of Troy off MT 56, is a splendid six-room, reconstructed log retreat on 100 acres complete with apple orchards, good ol' southern hospitality, and endless views of the picturesque Cabinet Mountains. On a ranch chock-full of lore, the McCrarys' retirement dream was to restore the original lodge and farmhouse while making their own additions, including a pond and hydropower. They have kept track of the comings and goings of the Swanson clan, which you can read while you're there.

Alternative Places to Bunk

Troy: The town of Troy rents a five-person yurt on the Kootenai River for $50 a night. The **Kootenai River Camp & Cabins** (406-295-4090) has tent and RV sites in the pines on the river and is open May through September. Cabins are $35 for two people and $60 for the larger one that sleeps seven; there are 25 hook-up RV sites and five tent sites.

Forest Service Cabins/Lookouts: (Reservations: 877-444-6777 or www.recreation.gov.) You've heard of rooms with a view? For views with a room, rent a forest-fire lookout. The Kootenai National Forest (406-293-6211) has more for rent than any forest in the Pacific Northwest—nine, including seven accessed from the Yaak-Koocanusa Route: The 45-foot-high **Yaak Mountain Lookout** ($35/sleeps four) near Troy, 41-foot **Big Creek Baldy Lookout** ($35/sleeps four) near Turner Mountain Ski Area, 40-foot **Mount Baldy/Buckhorn Ridge Lookout** ($35/sleeps four) west of Yaak, and 40-foot **Garver Mountain Lookout** ($35/sleeps four) northwest of Yaak. For cabins, primitive **McGuire Mountain** ($25/sleeps four) off MT 37 between Libby and Rexford has views of Lake Koocanusa and the Purcell Mountains, the spacious **Upper Ford Cabin** ($50/sleeps seven) just northeast of Yaak is accessible year-round on pavement, and **Webb Mountain Lookout** ($35/sleeps five) is a cabin 10 feet off the ground with views of Lake Koocanusa as well as Glacier National Park's highest peaks. Most lookouts and cabins are equipped with spartan beds, mattresses, and propane cook stoves. Some cabins are equipped with bathrooms, but the towers only have separate one-holers. These are extremely popular, especially in summer; for lookouts in particular, book well in advance.

Best Eats

Libby: The only town on the route with the usual fast-food suspects, Libby also provides some diversity. The best breakfast stop in town is the **Libby Café** ($, 406-293-3523 B/L), popular for its Montana Muffins (which can be shipped back home); it was for sale in early 2011. Like many bakeries in Montana, the Libby Café takes advantage of the state's most famous local berry: the huckleberry, which only grows in the wild. Have the huckleberry flapjacks for breakfast and take a few huckleberry swirls (gooey treats) for the road. **Fiesta Bonita** ($$, 406-293-6687, L/D) has authentic Mexican food (*muy bueno* fajitas) and refreshing wine margaritas. For a night in, rent a video and get a cooked or take-and-bake pizza from **Pizza & A Movie** ($$, 406-293-7492, D, Mon.–Sat.). The pizzas are laden with toppings and named after such movies as ET, Casa Blanca, and Titanic (which is loaded). **Red Dog Saloon & Pizza** ($/$$, 406-293-8347, L/D), north of town on the way to Turner Mountain Ski Area, is one of those great family-friendly, community-gossip-gathering, peanut-shells-on-the-floor bars/eateries—with a decent pizza to boot. Also worth a try is rustic Antlers ($$, 406-293-6464, B/L/D), which has a little bit of everything American.

Yaak: To get a glimpse of the mining days of the Yaak, grab a drink at the **Golden Nugget** ($$, 406-295-4433, D), which is pretty much in the sticks, about halfway between Yaak and Troy. The place was formerly a ball mill, and the crushing equipment is still there. The Golden Nugget is a favored watering hole among the area's eclectic residents; the dinner schedule is dependent on whether the cook shows up. The saloon can be a raucous place on any given evening, sometimes with live music. Believe it or not, reservations are recommended for their periodic fish-fry dinners.

Troy: Jack's Café ($, 406-295-4352, B/L) does little on the exterior to coax you in, and there's nothing special on the interior, either. Oh, and the owner/cook can be a bit crusty. But can she ever cook! And you won't believe the prices. Breakfasts are what you'd expect—no trimmings, but they hit the spot. Her Friday night prime-rib dinner for less than $10 brings folks out of the woods. If you show up late, you're probably out of luck; you'll just have to come back for breakfast.

The Dirty Shame Saloon in Yaak is decidedly tamer than it once was, but it's still a Montana icon.

Best Bar

Yaak: Time was, the **Dirty Shame Saloon** was one of the roughest, toughest bars in all of Montana. Loggers, shut-ins, rawhide Forest Service workers, and even airmen from the now-defunct Yaak Air Force Base stumbled into the remote bar after hours, all looking for a stiff drink and, in many cases, a fight. The saloon's name was reportedly coined by one of the airmen who frequented what was then called the Yaak River Lodge. It was, he said, "a dirty shame" that the place looked nothing like an actual lodge.

Another legend has it that the great boxer Joe Louis once ordered a scotch at the bar, and when told they didn't have it, he reputedly replied, "That's a dirty shame." Why—or if—Joe Louis was actually in Yaak is lost to the dustbin of history.

These days, the Dirty Shame is no longer dirty, but still a Montana classic. The old woodstove stands guard inside, and a scan of the interior reveals a few bullet holes left over from the renovation, each with a gritty story. New owners Don and Gloria Belcher, the former a Maryland clergyman and the latter a retired stockbroker, have cleaned up the joint—so much so that many former regulars refuse to patronize it. It's borderline bistro.

Gloria cheerily tends to the place; she schedules musician and author visits and has raised the food bar dramatically. She serves a Sunday buffet breakfast from 8 AM to noon, which includes scrumptious corned beef hash, Belgian waffles, fried red potatoes, and loads more—juice and coffee included—for $8. Supper is served until 3 PM Sundays, when she closes early for a rest. The rest of the week, it's breakfast, lunch (try the pastrami Reuben), and dinner at the usual times, except for Thursdays—going-to-town day—when she closes. If you eat too much, take a hike and come back for her chocolate dessert or Yaak sundaes, especially the huckleberry when available. If the weather isn't cooperating with your hiking or exploration plans, draw a draft and settle into 25-cent pool games. It's so different, the saloon probably warrants a name change—but with all its history, that would be a dirty shame.

LIBBY STILL REELING FROM ASBESTOS SCARE

Looking at Libby, with its forested hillsides and dramatic Cabinet Mountain Wilderness backdrop, it's difficult to imagine that this visually arresting community on the banks of the Kootenai River could be the site of the nation's first and only public health emergency. Yet that's just the case, thanks to the town's ongoing issues with vermiculite contamination from an unusually toxic form of asbestos from a nearby mine that closed in 1990.

From the 1920s to 1990, the Libby mine produced up to 80 percent of the world's vermiculite on Zonolite Mountain, 6 miles north of town. Along the way, however, Libby and nearby Troy suffered from an extraordinarily high rate of such lung diseases as asbestosis or the lethal mesothelioma because of a fine white dust that coated mine workers and, when the winds blew right, the entire town. Just how serious the health issue was didn't fully become public until 1999, after an investigative report by the *Seattle Post-Intelligencer* and then a one-man crusade by a terminally ill miner named Les Skramstad. Nearly every family in a valley of 12,000 people has been directly affected. They have contracted diseases in many ways, ranging from direct contact by miners to wives inhaling it off laundry and kids playing on vermiculite-coated piles near the baseball field.

This led to a massive cleanup, and in 2002, Libby was added to the Environmental Protection Area's list of federal Superfund sites. In the past decade, more than 1,100 residential and commercial properties have been cleaned up, with more still needing help. In 2009, the EPA declared a health emergency, stating that the job was far from over and that the residents of Libby needed more help to recover from a decades-long tragedy. Another $130 million was made available for medical aid and cleanup.

Is it safe to spend time in Libby today? Depends on who you ask; the tragedy has divided the town between those who are angry and those who fear economic devastation due to the asbestos stigma. Certainly, a great deal of cleanup remains, but a 2008 EPA study showed the air in Libby is safe. Passing through town or using Libby as a base to explore the Yaak/Koocanusa region is no cause for concern. And the resilient people who have suffered all these years will appreciate your support.

The Perfect Weekend

Arriving in Troy on a Friday night, check into the **Troy Montana Log Cabins** on the west end of town on US 2. In the morning, don't let the ruddy exterior of **Jack's Café** in Troy deter you from a great breakfast at a great price. After downing a last cup of coffee, stop at the US 2 roadside and take the short hike over the steel walking bridge above the railroad tracks to gape at the magnificent **Kootenai Falls**. Arriving in Libby in the late morning, spend some time wandering **The Heritage Museum**, which features a steam locomotive and a retrospective of the deadly 1910 fires that ravaged northwest Montana and northern Idaho. You might be tempted to have a second breakfast at the **Libby Café**, but the lunches are equally appealing. About 18 miles after leaving Libby, take a tour of the massive **Libby Dam** (summers), which creates Lake Koocanusa. Now settle in for a picturesque drive along the lake's shore—we suggest the wilder western flank on paved FS 228. Follow the shoreline and the winding forest roads into the Yaak River headwaters, then continue to the community of Yaak. Check into the rustic **Yaak River Cabins** at the **Dirty Shame Saloon**, definitely the place for drinks and dinner. Stick around in the morning for the breakfast buffet, then head south on the Yaak River Road to **Yaak River Falls**. Continue back to Troy and, if you're still in the mood for exploration, venture south 20 miles on MT 56 for a hike amid the **Ross Giant Cedars**. Return to Troy and then Libby, and dinner at **Red Dog Saloon & Pizza** on Pipe Creek Road 6 miles north of Libby.

DETOUR: ONE FOR THE ROAD

The Flathead Valley
Ravalli to Bigfork

Estimated length: 71 miles

Highlights: Flathead Indian Reservation, National Bison Range, St. Ignatius Mission, Ninepipe National Wildlife Refuge, Ninepipes Museum of Early Montana, The People's Center, Pablo National Wildlife Refuge, cherry orchards, Mission Mountain Winery, Flathead Lake State Park's Finley Point and Yellow Bay units.

Getting there: From I-90's Exit 96 just west of Missoula, the Flathead is a brisk 30-mile drive north on MT 93. You'll go 7 miles on four-lane highway over a small pass through Arlee to Ravalli and continue north 3 more miles to St. Ignatius. From the west, take I-90's Exit 33 at St. Regis and follow the Clark Fork River east on MT 135 to the junction of MT 200. Turn east along the Flathead River through Dixon to Ravalli.

In a state renowned for its awe-inspiring mountain vistas, the mighty Mission Mountains epitomize the term *majestic* more than any other. The Missions aren't Montana's highest mountains. Or longest. Or most rugged. Yet there is a mystique about the Missions, due perhaps to their wildness, or their grizzly bear study area, or most likely because of the way they rise abruptly from the Flathead Valley to heights of close to 10,000 feet. Remarkably, these towering mountains are only about 10 miles across, from the east side of Flathead Lake to MT 83 in the Swan Valley.

The Missions form the backdrop for the entire length of this drive through the rapidly growing area between Missoula and Kalispell. Much of the route goes through the 1.2-million-acre **Flathead Indian Reservation**, shared by the Salish, Kootenai, and Pend d'Oreille tribes.

The reservation is an extraordinary story in that it's the only one of seven in Montana that enjoys some prosperity. Indeed, except for road signs in the native tongue and the tribal headquarters, the unsuspecting visitor would be hard-pressed to know the difference between Indian and Anglo lands. The reasons for this uncommon prosperity are many, mostly an economic diversity that includes a willingness to sell reservation lands to non-Indians. The tribes have also demonstrated some foresight: They were the first in the nation to designate part of their reservation as wilderness; much of the Mission Mountains southeast of Flathead Lake remain as wild as they were 150 years ago. If you want to explore the Mission Mountain Wilderness or fish in some of the reservation's beautiful trout waters, such as the Jocko or Flathead rivers or the Ninepipe National Wildlife Refuge, you'll need to pick up a special permit from tribal recreation headquarters in Pablo.

Because Indians and bison are synonymous, it's fitting that soon after arriving on the reservation at **Ravalli** (pop. 119) the **National Bison Range** comes into view. To access one of the country's oldest wildlife refuges, drive west from Ravalli on MT 200 to Dixon and north on County Road 212 to the headquarters at **Moiese**. There are two driving loops—an easy 5-mile route on gravel through a bison pasture and the more involved but more scenic 19-mile Red Sleep Mountain Drive on gravel with occasional steep switchbacks. The area was literally one of the last refuges for the American bison, which once thundered across the plains in the tens of millions but were reduced to about two dozen in the late 1800s. About 350 to 500 roam there now, remnants of a wild herd from the Blackfeet country and a potential source for starting new wild herds.

Back on US 93, the highway bends northeast from Ravalli toward **St. Ignatius** (pop. 788), site of Montana's first Indian school and home to the wonderfully preserved and ornate **St. Ignatius Mission**. Step inside and marvel at the murals on the ceiling of the 1891 building, constructed with more than 1 million bricks; the murals were painted by the mission's cook.

At St. Ignatius the valley broadens and US 93 cuts an almost straight line north to **Charlo** (pop. 439) and the **Ninepipe National Wildlife Refuge**. On the left side is Ninepipe Reservoir, on the right Kicking Horse Reservoir, both key stopovers on a major flyway for migratory waterfowl. To learn more about the tribes, stop at the **Ninepipes Museum of Early**

Montana next to the refuge. Continuing north, you'll pass through **Ronan** (pop. 1,968) en route to **Pablo** (pop. 1,814) and tribal headquarters. **The People's Center** is a museum-plus, with Indian exhibits, programs, and tribal-led tours called Native Ed-Ventures. Just past Pablo on the west is the **Pablo National Wildlife Refuge,** another sanctuary for migrating birds.

Up next is **Polson** (pop. 5,046), where Flathead Lake comes into view. With 180 miles of shoreline, Flathead Lake is the largest freshwater lake in the western United States. The Flathead River empties into the northern end of the lake and leaves just west of Polson, which has two fun museums and a decidedly destination-vacation atmosphere. The **Miracle of America Museum** has a transportation emphasis and is full of surprises, including a 65-foot caricature of Paul Bunyan among its more than 100,000 items. A more traditional museum is the **Polson-Flathead Historical Museum**; it has a cluttered collection of homesteading artifacts and also boasts Nessie the Flathead Monster—the mount of a 181-pound sturgeon caught in the lake. A great evening diversion is the Port Polson Players, on display during the summers at the **Polson Performing Arts Center.**

At Polson, you'll have two options for skirting Flathead Lake: US 93 continues around the west side of the lake and MT 35 hugs the eastern shores. Neither will disappoint, but we recommend the eastern route through the cherry orchards for which the Flathead is famous (unless you want a wine fix, in which case Dayton on the west shore is home to **Mission Mountain Winery,** one of two in the state, along with Missoula's Ten Spoon). The routes rejoin at Somers on the north shore of Flathead Lake for the 10-mile drive into Kalispell.

Heading east on MT 35 toward the Missions, you're quickly in cherry country, featuring dozens of varieties. If you want to catch the cherry trees in bloom, come early to mid-May. The cherry harvest is typically from mid-July to mid-August, and roadside stands are seemingly in every wide spot in the road.

Flathead Lake State Park comprises six units, including Finley Point and Yellow Bay on the east side. Finley Point features a 16-site campground amid tall pines and cherry orchards on a skinny arm that juts into the lake—ideal for launching a boat and fishing. Yellow Bay is farther north on MT 35, and its five campsites accommodate people who come to pick the cherries in nearby orchards. Another 10 wooded miles north is Woods Bay, the last tiny hamlet before the trendy and touristy **Bigfork** (see Seeley-Swan route).

Red jammer buses offer open-air views of Glacier's splendor, plus interpretive services. National Park Service

CHAPTER

8

Mountains and Majesty: The Going-to-the-Sun Loop

West Glacier/St. Mary/East Glacier/Essex

Estimated length: 132 miles
Estimated time: 7 hours to 2 days (summer/fall)

Highlights: Wildlife viewing, hiking, Middle Fork of the Flathead River, Lake McDonald, Bird Woman Falls, Weeping Wall, Logan Pass, St. Mary Lake, Two Medicine, Marias Pass, Walton Goat Lick Overlook, Essex.

Getting there: The fastest way to Glacier National Park from I-90 is the US 93 exit west of Missoula. Take US 93 north to Ravalli and continue through the Flathead Indian Reservation to Polson. US 93 continues around the west side of shimmering Flathead Lake. You can skirt the traffic through Kalispell by taking County Road 206 around the southeast end of town to the junction of US 2 west of Columbia Falls. From there, it's 16 four-lane miles through the eclectic mountain towns of Hungry Horse, Martin City, and Coram into West Glacier.

From Missoula, take MT 200 east through Ovando and Lincoln over Rogers Pass to the junction of US 287, then turn north. Stay on US 287 until it meets US 89 at Choteau, and continue northwest on US 89 to Browning, where three roads lead to Glacier National Park. Another way is to leave I-90 at Butte and travel north on I-15 through Helena to Wolf Point, where US 287 veers to the north and begins the Rocky Mountain Front tour to Browning.

Glacier International Airport in Kalispell is served by Delta, Horizon, United Express, and Allegiant. Amtrak's Empire Builder has one stop daily each direction at East Glacier, Essex, and West Glacier.

Overview

Only one highway in Montana—the Beartooth between Red Lodge and Cooke City—can match the Going-to-the-Sun Road in Glacier National Park for sheer jaw-dropping magnificence. This dramatic cliff-hugging ribbon of pavement surely leads the state in photo-ops per mile, whether it's for the grandeur of its serrated mountain peaks, the sweeping views of U-shaped valleys, a distant glacier shimmering under a bright sun, or people-tolerant mountain goats nibbling on the grasses peeking through snows.

Here, slightly south of the Canadian border, the Rockies are squeezed into a 50-mile-wide spine, forced skyward by the prairie on the east and Flathead Valley on the west. The Blackfeet who roamed this sacred country called it "The Backbone of the World." Early conservationist George Bird Grinnell labeled it "The Crown of the Continent."

Slightly more than a century ago, the park was the similar but separate vision of both the naturalist Grinnell and a railroad tycoon named James J. Hill, albeit for polar opposite reasons. Grinnell saw a national park as a way to preserve unparalleled beauty and a precious source of water spilling off the Crown toward the Atlantic, Pacific, and Arctic oceans; for Hill, it was a marketing tool to lure passengers west on his Great Northern Railroad. "See America first" was Hill's rallying cry in coaxing Easterners to explore a last vestige of untamed wilderness. Hill envisioned an American Swiss Alps without livestock and villages, and dreamed of building magnificent chalet-style hotels in the wilderness. Today, those chalets are as much a part of Glacier's persona as pointy mountains and ice fields.

In 1910, less than a decade after a park was first seriously proposed, Glacier joined the National Park System. "See it before it's gone," the Great Northern implored in its advertisements, referring to the wilderness and the choreographed routines of the Blackfeet that Hill placed in the park (see sidebar). Today, the same mantra applies, only to the park's namesake feature—the glacier. Over millions of years, glaciers have come and gone, and they have been melting since about 1850. But global warming has accelerated the pace to such a degree that climate models show the remaining 23 disappearing within a decade. Now is indeed the time to see them before they're gone—though even without glaciers, this region will retain its grandeur.

Going-to-the-Sun is the only road bisecting the park, and it's an experience not to be missed. As you'll soon understand, the 48.7-mile road was an engineering marvel when completed in 1932 after 11 years of construction. It was conceived in 1917, the result of a mandate to make parks accessible to a newfangled contraption called the automobile. To this day, the road ranks at or near the top of the most challenging road-building projects in American history. Though one might guess that the name comes from the seeming rise to the sun at Logan Pass, it's actually a nod to a nearby mountain—named for a Blackfeet legend about a celestial being called Sour Spirit, who would come down from the sky to assist the tribe in dire times and go back to the sun when his mission was accomplished.

The marvel today is keeping the road over 6,646-foot Logan Pass open. Plowing snow as deep as 80 feet requires up to 10 weeks. Beginning in 2009, the National Park Service was in the process of a badly needed, decade-long road-restoration process that will demand patience. Expect delays of no more than 30 minutes even in the worst of circumstances, and where better to be idled anyway? Shut off your engine, step out of your car, breathe in the clean mountain air, and enjoy the vistas.

The grandeur doesn't end when the Going-to-the-Sun Road drops into St. Mary. The stretch through aspen and foothills to East Glacier on the eastern fringes of the Blackfeet Indian Reservation is also spectacular, and US 2 between East Glacier and West Glacier offers peeks at mountaintops while splitting Glacier and the Great Bear Wilderness Area.

Hitting the Road

In Glacier's early days, most visitors arrived via rail at **East Glacier** (pop. 396). Today the busiest entrance is West Glacier. Tourists still come by train on both sides, but air access to Kalispell, access from I-90, and the generally more aesthetically pleasing landscapes to the west have turned the blue-collar communities of **Kalispell** (pop. 14,223) and **Columbia Falls** (pop. 3,645) into working towns catering to tourists. Also alluring is **Whitefish** (pop. 11,526), a destination village not unlike Sun Valley or Vail that has a year-round economy due to the Whitefish Mountain Resort at Big Mountain ski area.

As you come toward **West Glacier** (pop. 426) from Kalispell or Columbia Falls, explore the canyon area or, as the locals call it, "up the line"—a reference to the string of one-time trapping communities between Columbia Falls and the park. **Hungry Horse** (pop. 934), **Coram** (pop. 684), and **Martin**

The Going-to-the-Sun Road

SCALE
0   5 Miles
0   5 KM

Alberta

Saskatchewan

CANADA
UNITED STATES

17   89

Glacier
National
Park

Babb

Cattle Baron
Supper Club

89

Polebridge

Blackfeet
Indian
Reservation

Park Cafe
St. Mary
Snowgoose Grille

GOING-TO-THE-SUN RD

Logan
Pass

Jackson
Glacier
Overlook

St. Mary
Lake

89

Lake
McDonald

Lake
McDonald
Lodge

Eddie's

Apgar

West Glacier

Belton
Chalet

Browning

89

49

2

Whitefish

Coram

Martin City

Hungry
Horse

Brownie's,
Glacier Park Lodge

East Glacier

2

Columbia
Falls

2

Izaak
Walton
Inn

Essex

2

2

Kalispell

35

93

35

Hungry Horse
Reservoir

Montana

Bigfork

93   35   83

Flathead
Lake

N FORK RD

CAMAS RD

Flathead River

Middle Fork Flathead River

City (pop. 424) are home to a once-reclusive and sometimes-lawless collection of folks who came to help build the Hungry Horse Dam on the South
Fork of the Flathead River—and never left. Today, these towns have mel-
lowed with an influx of new blood, and are more inviting to tourists.

As you approach the loop's beginnings in West Glacier, you'll know
you're in a national park gateway community. Motels, campgrounds,
lodges, helicopter tours, rafting companies, trading posts, and an assort-

ment of Coney Island-esque activities are the giveaways. That doesn't mean some aren't redeeming. For a mountain state, Montana is surprisingly shy of whitewater rafting thrills, but the Middle Fork of the Flathead River provides some of the best Class III splash-and-giggle runs in the state; no fewer than three outfitters in West Glacier offer day trips.

West Glacier itself has retained a pre–World War II feel with its throwback shops, restaurant, bar, motel, and cabins. In fact, the company that owns the businesses in West Glacier and Apgar is responsible for avoiding the cheap T-shirt and cheesy-photograph environments that plague so many national park gateway towns.

On US 2 at West Glacier, once called Belton, cross the Middle Fork to the village of **Apgar** (pop. 426), which sits at the southern end of picturesque, glacier-carved **Lake McDonald** and is home to the park's headquarters. Before starting the Going-to-the-Sun Road into the park's interior, consider a detour on the 23-mile paved and gravel Inside Road along the astonishingly wild North Fork of the Flathead River. It leads to the commune-ish village of **Polebridge** (pop. 90) and its rustic mercantile, home of the best fresh-baked bread and bear claws in the region. The only public bathroom is a one-holer behind the mercantile, but it adds to the charm.

Apgar Village signals the beginning of the Going-to-the-Sun Road, which hugs the forested shores of 470-foot-deep Lake McDonald before beginning its precipitous rise to the sun and then making a less-dramatic descent to the aspen, pine, and prairie at St. Mary.

The road is so spectacular you might want to leave the driving to someone else. The park offers free shuttles between West Glacier and St. Mary that run every 15 to 30 minutes, with strategically located stops along the way. For an informative guided trip, consider **Red Bus Tours** (406-892-2525 U.S., 403-236-3400 Canada), a concessionaire under the name Glacier Park Inc. that runs half-day and full-day tours in the historic, open-topped red "jammer" buses—so named because the buses once had standard transmissions and drivers could be heard "jamming" the gears—starting at $30 per person and capping at $83, depending on your tour choice. Different dates are assigned to each tour, but basically the jammers run June through mid-September, with the exception of the Huckleberry Mountain Tour, which begins in late May or early June and ends in September. These environmentally friendly buses run on 93 percent propane.

From Apgar, the road is mostly straight as it rises gently along the lake's shore to the chalet-style **Lake McDonald Lodge** (May–Sept.) and past Avalanche Creek for about 25 miles until you reach The Loop. To fully appreciate the park's forested lower-elevation areas, stop after the **Avalanche Creek Campground** and hike the **Trail of the Cedars**, a boardwalk amid an ancient grove of western red cedars, hemlocks, and yews—Montana's version of a rain forest. Shortly after Avalanche Creek, the road makes a sharp left turn and begins emerging from the pines, cedars, and firs toward the pass. Every break in the trees offers one breathtaking view after another as the glacier-carved Lake McDonald Valley grows ever deeper.

As you continue to elevate, look for many of the glacial landforms that give the park its character. Straight ahead you'll see the **Garden Wall**, a vertical rock face called an *arête* that was created as glaciers on both sides of the Continental Divide scraped away at the mountains. Look also for high-elevation meadows called hanging gardens, the result of little glaciers being unable to keep up with the work of larger glaciers below. Also prominent are the bowls at the head of glaciers, called cirques. After navigating the road's lone substantial switchback at The Loop, the road opens to a sweeping view of 492-foot **Bird Woman Falls** across the valley, eases under the **Weeping Wall**—where a waterfall lands on the road, its volume dependent upon the season—and **Big Bend**, perhaps the most popular viewpoint on the west side of Logan Pass. Just past Big Bend is **Triple Arches**, the best stone-and-mortar example of the massive challenge faced by Depression-era road builders.

Crowds notwithstanding, you'll want to spend a few hours at **Logan Pass**, the road's climax. Open mid-June through mid-October, the **Logan Pass Visitor Center** (406-888-7800) is where you'll learn about the fragile plant and animal life at high elevations before striking out on one of the two hikes that depart from the summit. The 6-mile **Hidden Lake Nature Trail** on pavement, boardwalk, and then gravel is the park's most popular hike. Bring a fly rod to fish for Yellowstone cutthroat trout in the lake. Across the road from the visitors center, the **Highline Trail** cuts across the Garden Wall and isn't for the weak-kneed—for about 100 yards early in the hike there is a sheer drop off, and you might have to—or get to, depending on your perspective—share the trail with a single-minded mountain goat.

Heading down the east side of Logan Pass, you'll notice a drier forest with more pine, aspen, and eventually sagebrush. Highlights of the backside include the 408-foot **East Tunnel** through Piegan Mountain and a stop at the **Jackson Glacier Overlook**, 4 miles below the pass. This is the only place on the road where a glacier is still visible; snap a photo and then com-

Mountain goats make the knee-wobbling Highline Trail look easy.

pare the current size of the glacier to visitors center pictures from the 1930s, 1950s, and even 1980s. Look to the north side of the road, and you'll see its namesake mountain, Going-to-the-Sun, which rises to 9,642 feet. The road down to **St. Mary Lake** offers a number of worthwhile short hikes, including an easy 3.6-mile round-tripper to St. Mary and Virginia falls, a short walk to 75-foot **Sunrift Gorge**, and the 1.2-mile **Sun Point Nature Trail** to views of the lake. One more stop to make is at the **Wild Goose Island Overlook**, where a tiny island is a striking contrast in St. Mary Lake against a mountain backdrop.

Five miles before St. Mary is **Rising Sun** (866-875-8456, mid-June–mid-Sept.), which offers the first services since Lake McDonald, including boat rides across the lake. Take a look around at the prairie and aspen landscape and ponder just how much it has changed in the 35 miles since the ancient cedars on the west side. St. Mary has a visitors center and a con-

Marias Pass, the only year-round crossing of the Northern Rockies between Canada and Rogers Pass near Helena, has memorials to J. F. Stevens and Slippery Bill Morrison.

gested conglomeration of restaurants, motels, gas stations, and gift shops.

Turn right on US 89 for the pretty 33-mile drive through aspen and sage foothills toward East Glacier, keeping an eye on the majestic mountains visible on the passenger's side. Look for Blackfeet ponies high on benches in scenes reminiscent of 150 years ago. At a little outpost called Kiowa, turn right on MT 49 for 13 miles of zigging and zagging through the

Two Medicine country to **East Glacier** (pop. 396), which has a few smaller motels, motor inns, eateries and gift shops, an Amtrak station, and the massive **Glacier Park Lodge**.

Just under the railroad bridge is the junction of US 2, which begins a quick if not as dramatic ascent to 5,220-foot **Marias Pass** to the west. The views at the summit—including 8,770-foot Summit Mountain to the north—are enticing. Pull into a large parking area that features a miniature version of the Washington Monument dedicated to J. F. Stevens. He was a Great Northern Railway engineer who discovered the route across the Rockies with the help of a Blackfeet scout. Also at the pass is a tribute to a Slippery Bill Morrison, who donated a portion of his 160-acre spread to create the only year-round passage through the Rockies between Rogers Pass and the Canadian border.

When US 2 descends to the Flathead River and bends north, look for the **Walton Goat Lick Overlook** on the left side. A short walk to a viewing platform reveals a natural salt lick where as many as 50 mountain goats at a time, as well as bighorn sheep, deer, and other wildlife, regularly convene for an energy boost. A few miles beyond are the communities of **Walton** and **Essex** (pop. 223), where the extravagant **Izaak Walton Inn** is worth exploring even if you're not staying in one of its railroad-oriented lodging options. The 29-room hotel, often called Inn Between because of its location between East Glacier and West Glacier, was built as a possible southern entrance for Glacier. The hotel has survived numerous disappointments and evolved to become a destination for visitors desiring unusual year-round lodging. It has become a twice-daily hotel tradition to wander onto the porch to wave at Amtrak passengers.

The next 25 miles offer some of the wildest paved-road country in America. Glacier rises above the Flathead River on the north side and the Great Bear Wilderness looms on the south.

Best Places to Bunk

Hungry Horse: The **Tamarack Lodge & Cabins** ($/$$, 406-387-4420) is a bit off the beaten byway, but it's open year-round and has a historic appeal while still providing excellent park access.

West Glacier: The closest thing the Glacier area has to an all-inclusive environment is the **Great Northern Resort** ($$/$$$$, 800-735-7897),

Stay in an intimate room at the Izaak Walton Hotel, near Essex—or in a refurbished railcar on the grounds.

which in addition to lodging offers whitewater rafting, kayak instruction, fly-fishing trips, and a host of other activities. The double-decked log A-frames with a Swiss motif come in two sizes: small sleeping four to six and large sleeping six to eight. The immaculate **Heaven's Peak Lodge & Resort** ($$$$, 406-387-4754), which caters to wedding parties and small groups, is the most luxurious lodging in the area and has the rates to match. The highly appealing **Belton Chalet** ($$/$$$, 406-888-235-8665, Dec.–Oct.) opened in 1910 when the park was christened and calls itself "the way it was…and still is." The 25 hotel rooms shutter during the fall, winter, and spring, but the two cottages remain open and are a bargain in the winter at $99. Sixteen miles east on US 2 is the family-oriented **Stanton Creek Lodge Bar & Café** ($/$$, 406-888-5040, May–Oct.), which boasts the lowest rates on US 2 with their six cozy but cute cabins and eight RV spots. They also have a café that serves lunch and dinner—including a very tasty buffalo burger—all for under $10.

Apgar Village: Towering old-growth cedars provide ambience for **Apgar Village Lodge** ($$/$$$, 406-888-5484, May–Sept.), a rustically maintained complex of 28 cabins (26 with kitchens) and 20 motel rooms on the shores of Lake McDonald. Eleven miles inside the park, three-story **Lake McDonald Lodge** ($$$, 866-875-8456, May–Sept.), the most requested lodging in the park, is a perfect example of the original Swiss chalet architecture. The historic 1914 hotel has 100 total rooms, including 38 cabins on the shores of the aquamarine waters of its namesake lake. There is also a two-story motor inn with 30 rooms in the pines out back.

St. Mary: Of all of the Glacier-area hotels, the 1932 **St. Mary Lodge & Resort** ($$$/$$$$, 888-778-6279, May–Sept.) best mixes the old and the new, with upscale digs and family lodging. The 142-room hotel rises above the congestion in St. Mary and provides stunning views of St. Mary Lake and the mountains from its third-floor rooms. Also a part of the property is the even more posh 48-room **Great Bear Lodge**, which opened in 2001 and is a modern version of the classic park hotels with decidedly luxurious rooms; also available are renovated 1937 cabins and 27 comfy teepees. Five miles up the Going-to-the-Sun Road, the **Rising Sun Motor Inn & Cabins** ($$, 406-892-2925, June–Sept.) features some of the more affordable family lodging in the area with 72 rooms and cabins. Rising Sun, which overlooks St. Mary Lake, has survived a 2009 interior fire that damaged some rooms.

East Glacier: Looming above the rest, literally, is the **Glacier Park Lodge** ($$/$$$$, 406-892-2525, May–Sept.), the most attractive and alluring of the Swiss-style chalets built by the Great Northern Railway a century ago. Few folks come to Glacier to golf, but the lodge has a course—plus a swimming pool for entertaining restless kids. If the lodge is a bit out of your budget, the cleanest and most appealing options among the many family-owned operations north of the village are **Jacobson's Cottages** ($, 406-226-4422, May–Oct.) and the **Mountain Pines Motor Inn** ($, 406-226-4403, May–Sept.); be sure to get reservations early.

Essex: The year-round **Izaak Walton Inn** ($/$$$$, 406-888-5700) is a historic marvel, with 29 rooms in the two-story hotel plus four cabooses and a locomotive that have been converted into deluxe accommodations.

Alternative Bunking

Camping: The **West Glacier KOA** (406-387-5341, May–Oct.) is well-kept, has a heated pool and hot tubs, and is set amid enough pine trees to provide a sense of peace and quiet. Not far away, the 175-site **Glacier Campground** (406-387-5689, May–Oct.) is no-frills camping on 40 acres surrounded by the wooded Flathead National Forest. The 700-square-foot teepees at **St. Mary Lodge** (888-778-6279, May–Sept.) don't have electricity, but they do come with queen beds and a bathhouse with Jacuzzi tub. The **East Glacier KOA** (406-732-4122, May–Oct.), across the St. Mary River from US 89 on the west shore of St. Mary Lake, offers splendid views of the mountains; a new swimming pool and bocce court add to the fun.

Forest Service Cabins/Lookouts: (Reservations: 877-444-6777 or www.recreation.gov.) Off the beaten byway, but worth the backwoods drive into the Flathead National Forest, is the year-round **Ben Rover Cabin** (406-758-5204, $50/sleeps eight) along the Wild and Scenic North Fork of the Flathead River outside tiny Polebridge. You get more than the usual Forest Service amenities at Ben Rover—propane stove and heat, lights, firewood, utensils, water from an outdoor well pump, and a living-room view of Glacier forest. Also north of Polebridge is the Forest Service's year-round **Wurtz Cabin** (406-758-5204, $50/sleeps eight). For a seriously primitive experience, the 1922 **Hornet Lookout** (406-758-5204, $20/sleeps four, June–Nov.) is literally a (rustic) room with a (spectacular) view not far from the Wurtz Cabin.

Best Eats

Coram: The **Packers Roost** (406-387-5533, B/L/D) isn't as tough as it looks—or once was—and is a great place to grab a bite and a brew and get a feel for the diverse canyon lifestyles. You'll need three hands for the burger, and you might be surprised to learn this is also a cybercafé where you can get your daily dose of the *New York Times* with your morning coffee. Oh, and you can camp out back here, too—no charge.

West Glacier: Belton Grill Dining & Tap Room ($/$$$, 406-888-5000, D) makes every effort to provide local foods for a summer menu that ranges from salmon and stuffed veal to Montana Delmonico steak and

Packers Roost in Coram was once a rough-and-tumble joint "up the line."

duck agnolotti. And then there are the breakfasts—how about French toast with plaintains and cream cheese, drizzled with Kahlua and rum syrup. The acclaimed restaurant and taproom close in the fall and then reopen December through March with weekend service featuring appetizers (elk sliders), sandwiches (catfish po-boy), and entrées (pork medallions or chili salt-crusted walleye).

Apgar Village: Eddie's Restaurant, Gifts & Grocery ($$, 406-888-5361, B/L/D, May–Sept.) is the place to fill up on home-style cooking, ice-cream treats, specialty coffee drinks, huckleberry desserts, and snacks for the road before heading into the park. Daily dinner specials might include broasted chicken, rib eye, halibut, or trout—just what a hungry hiker needs.

RAILROAD MAGNATE MADE INDIANS PART OF GLACIER VISION

Great Northern Railroad president James J. Hill had a unique idea when he schemed to create a new national park in 1910.

As part of Hill's grand vision for what would be called Glacier National Park, he wouldn't banish the Blackfeet who lived on the nearby plains. No, he would *welcome* them. In what the *New York Times* labeled "Tourism of Doom," Hill's brilliant see-it-before-it's-gone marketing plan included luring nostalgic tourists west on his railroad by touting a vanishing wilderness—most notably the last place to see real Indians living much as they had before the western migration changed their lives forever. The Blackfeet hunted wild animals, rode their ponies, slipped into teepees at night, and moved in and out of the park's shadows.

In addition to moving freely across the eastern flanks of the park as they had for centuries, the Blackfeet also served as greeters at the train station in Midvale (now East Glacier), at the massive Swiss-style lodges, and at other key tourist spots. At many places, they sang, danced, and told Blackfeet stories for eastern tourists who couldn't get enough of this faux frontier.

This exotic marriage between the Anglo culture and Indians lasted about two decades, until the stock-market crash of 1929. Short of funds for advertising and marketing, the railroad no longer could afford the Blackfeet, who were sent back to their neighboring reservation on the prairie. By the time the economy rebounded during World War II, the Going-to-the-Sun Road had been completed, and more tourists were entering the park from the west.

Historians concede that the railroad's use of the Blackfeet was blatant exploitation, but they note it did have one benefit: By singing, dancing, and telling stories, the tribe retained an oral history at a time when fellow tribes' traditions were disappearing. The Blackfeet have a bittersweet relationship with Glacier today, partly because they feel disenfranchised, partly because what few park jobs they have are largely menial, and partly because they still struggle with the concept of political boundaries drawn across sacred earth on which they have lived for centuries.

St. Mary: How can you resist a café whose motto is "strength in pie"? The **Park Cafe** (406-753-4482, B/L/D, June–Sept.) is a standout for its multicultural menu—energy-packed breakfasts, curried chicken salad, bison burger, fish tacos, peanut veggie wrap, or grilled tofu sandwich (yep, that bean curd stuff), any of which, with any luck, can be enjoyed at one of their three outdoor tables creekside. The **Snowgoose Grille** ($$/$$$, 888-

778-6279, B/L/D, May–Sept.) in the Great Bear Lodge has elk tenderloin, bison steaks, whitefish from the lake, pasta entrées, and vegetarian selections. For the best ice cream in the area, try the **Curly Bear Cafe & Ice Cream Parlor** (406-732-4431) next to the gas station.

Babb: A taste of Missoula came to Babb in the form of the funky **Two Sisters Café** ($$, 406-732-5535, L/D, June–Sept.), which sports license plates from around the world as well as all 50 states formed in the shape of America; try the spicy empanada, red burger (all-natural Montana beef burger loaded with toppings), or just be decadently wild with a slice of huckleberry pie à la mode, sprinkled with huckleberries. The **Cattle Baron Supper Club** ($$$/$$$$, 406-732-4033, D, May–Oct.) was once known as one of the toughest bars in Montana; now the riffraff have been chased out and it's a classic western saloon/restaurant known for its mountain-sized—some say best-in-the-world—beef and bison steaks. The dining area upstairs overlooks an artistic buffalo jump above the bar and Running Eagle Falls, dedicated to a Blackfeet warrior. The walls are lined with pictograph murals interpreting Blackfeet history, making for thoughtful reading.

East Glacier: Brownie's Grocery ($, 406-226-4426, B/L) features a deli and grocery beneath three hostel rooms at $25 a night. Bright and early each morning you'll find Glacier tourists getting their day started with French toast, eggs, and coffee on the patio at **The Whistle Stop Cafe,** where a full breakfast can be had for a song.

Essex: The **Dining Car Restaurant** ($$$, 406-888-5700, B/L/D) at the Izaak Walton Inn is one of the few places in the region open year-round and caters to seasonal outdoor activities amid an authentic railway ambience. Regardless of the season, much of the menu is local—elk, bison, trout, huckleberries, and, naturally, beef. This might be the first place you'll taste a bison French dip.

The Perfect Weekend

In a lodging world filled with numerous choices to fit a wide global audience, we suggest starting at the **Belton Chalet** simply because it's a Glacier original, with all its nostalgic charm. It also has a phenomenal restaurant. Come hungry so you can order as many delectable choices as possible at the **Belton Grill Dining & Tap Room** before retiring for the night in the lodge.

Remote Polebridge is home to a cluster of off-the-grid residents and a mercantile selling sought-after baked goods.

Awaken to savory breakfast at the grill or head to Apgar Village for a stack of buttermilk pancakes at **Eddie's**. Be sure to stretch your legs at **Lake McDonald Lodge** and enjoy the views of this glistening jewel. After driving a short distance, get a brisk walk in on the **Trail of the Cedars** before hopping back in your car for the every-turn-another-breathtaking-view drive to Logan Pass. Take your time on the ascent and stop to snap photos of **Bird Woman Falls,** the **Weeping Wall, Big Bend,** and **Triple Arches.** At **Logan Pass**, explore the visitors center, grab a snack, and take another hike, either on the **Hidden Lake Nature Trail** or knee-wobbling **Highline Trail.** On the way down the backside to St. Mary, stop at **Jackson Glacier Overlook** to get a last look at a vanishing icon. Other breaks could include the **Sunrift Gorge** and **Sunlight Nature Trail.** Take some time to wander around St. Mary. If you're in the mood for a sit-down, pricey dinner of elk tenderloin or bison steak, we suggest **The Snowgoose Grille** in the impressive Great Bear Lodge or a short drive to the **Cattle Baron Supper Club** in Babb. If you want a more casual but guaranteed-to-please meal, get in line at the **Park Café** (saving room for pie is a must). Take the shortcut on US 89 and MT 49 to East Glacier, and check into the historic **Glacier Park Lodge** for a crowning park lodging experience. After a hot breakfast at **The Whistle Stop Cafe,** turn west on US 2 for the ascent to **Marias Pass.** On the descent

from Marias, and after the highway meets the Middle Fork of the Flathead River, look for the pullout marking **Walton Goat Lick Overlook** on the left. Soon you'll arrive in Essex and the **Izaak Walton Inn**, an ideal place to take a lunch break, explore the railcars, and wave to the trains as they thunder past.

DETOUR: ONE FOR THE ROAD

The Seeley-Swan

Clearwater Crossing to Bigfork

Estimated length: 89 miles

Highlights: Seeley Lake, Blackfoot-Clearwater Wildlife Management Area, Salmon Lake, Clearwater Canoe Trail, Seeley Lake Game Preserve, Holland Lake Falls, Old Squeezer Loop Road, Swan River National Wildlife Refuge, Swan Lake.

Getting there: From the west, leave I-90 at Bonner (Exit 109) just a few miles east of Missoula and follow the Blackfoot River upstream to the junction of MT 83 at Clearwater Crossing. From the east, either turn off I-90 at Garrison (Exit 174) and go east on US 12 for 14 miles to Avon, then drive northwest on MT 141 about 33 miles to the junction of MT 200. From there, go west through Ovando for 24 miles to Clearwater Crossing. A sometimes faster route: Remain on I-90 to County Road 271 (Exit 154) at Drummond and drive north 22 miles through Helmsville to a meeting with MT 141. Continue on through Ovando to the junction with MT 83.

Nowhere in Montana—not even in Glacier National Park—is the work of glaciers so immediately and easily evident than along the Seeley-Swan scenic drive, a spectacular 90-mile-long corridor that could leave the unsuspecting visitor wondering if he or she had awakened in Minnesota. The towering Mission Mountains to the west and Bob Marshall Wilderness to the east quickly dispel that notion. Still, driving from the southern end of this route on MT 83, near **Seeley Lake** (pop. 1,436), has the feel of the Land of 10,000 Lakes, with one after another connected by the Clearwater River. It's called the Clearwater Chain of Lakes, and it contains anywhere from six to 24 lakes, depending on your perspective. They're popular with Montanans, especially motorboaters and water-skiers.

Even after ascending a small divide and leaving the lakes behind on the way to **Bigfork** (pop. 1,421), the Seeley-Swan carves a straight northwesterly swath through a valley that rivals the forested isolation of the remote Yaak Valley. Many Montanans think of this as the "deer route" because of the prolific populations of whitetails that linger near the highway, especially in the early morning and at dusk; special care is required when driving this beautiful stretch. The route culminates at Swan Lake and then Bigfork, an artsy community on the shores of giant Flathead Lake.

The drive begins innocuously enough at Clearwater Crossing, where the namesake river flows into the Blackfoot. Three miles into the drive, though, the area's natural richness becomes apparent. The **Blackfoot-Clearwater Wildlife Management Area**, known simply as "The Game Range" in local parlance, is 67,000 acres of forest and grasslands with more than 3,000 wintering elk, mule deer, and whitetail deer; it's the largest Montana Fish, Wildlife & Parks wildlife area in the state. Large elk herds are visible in the fall after arriving from the Bob Marshall Wilderness to spend the winter before returning to "The Bob" in the summer.

Once you've passed the smallish Elbow, Harpers, and Blanchard lakes, the largest of the Big Six in the chain of lakes, Salmon, soon comes into view on the driver's side. **Salmon Lake** has a 42-acre state park with 20 campsites and is one of the best places in Montana to see up to 200 loons. Also noteworthy here is the western larch, a common conifer tree across

Road construction in Glacier gives drivers an extra opportunity to take in incomparable views.

western Montana that turns yellow and sheds its needles in the fall. A mile past Salmon Lake is the turn for **Placid Lake**, three miles up North Placid Lake Road. The lake also features a state park with a campground; anglers know the lake for its prolific population of landlocked kokanee salmon. Back on MT 83, the town of Seeley Lake is the hub of the southern end of the valley, luring folks from across the West to stay in cozy cabins amid ponderosa pines and ply the shimmering waters of the town's namesake lake. For a good chuckle, note the sign on the cemetery just before arriving in town: "The Best Last Place." There are three Forest Service campgrounds on the lake, and the town has an attractive assortment of lakefront motels, cabins, lodges, and dining options to serve as bases for exploring the region.

Four miles north of town begins the **Clearwater Canoe Trail**, identified by a sign on MT 83 and a short drive to the Seeley Lake Ranger District. The river meanders away from the highway through a peaceful willow marsh with a wide variety of birds and other wildlife; the area adjoins the

Seeley Lake Game Preserve. No motors are allowed, and after 3.5 miles of paddling if you don't feel like making the return trip, you can always leave the canoe at Seeley Lake and hike back on a well-maintained trail. At the upper end of the Clearwater are three more lakes in short order: **Inez, Alva, and Rainy**. Each has fishing access, and Inez and Alva have Forest Service campgrounds. After Rainy Lake, lakes are still out there—most of them smaller and requiring some effort to reach. The largest is **Lindbergh Lake**, a 3-mile drive west on Lindbergh Lake Road. Lindbergh, which has a Forest Service campground as well, is part of the chain of lakes on the Swan River. A mile north of the Lindbergh Road turnoff is Holland Lake Road, which leads 3 miles east to Holland Lake and a 1.5-mile hike through fir, pine, and larch on the **Holland Lake Falls National Recreation Trail** to a spectacular cascade. **Holland Lake Lodge** overlooking the lake offers rustic lodging with dining.

Back on MT 83, the only town between Seeley Lake and Swan Lake is **Condon** (pop. 576). The Forest Service rents two primitive cabins here for folks interested in a pure backwoods experience: the Condon Work Center and Owl Creek Cabin. For lodging with a little more comfort, there's the **Standing Stones Bed & Breakfast**. From there, MT 83 continues a forested journey through national forestlands and onto the **Swan River State Forest**, which includes a unique wildlife-viewing experience on the **Old Squeezer Loop Road**. The hiking trails near the forest's headquarters are popular among birdwatchers. Farther north on MT 83, on the southern tip of picturesque Swan Lake, is the 1,568-acre **Swan River National Wildlife Refuge**, created in 1973 as another sanctuary for migrating waterfowl.

Swan Lake is nearly 20 miles long and is known to fishermen for its kokanee, northern pike, and trout. The little village of **Swan Lake** has become popular for its more than 50 miles of groomed Nordic skiing trails and two campgrounds north of town.

After traveling the east side of the lake for 20 miles and passing through **Ferndale**, MT 83 bends left and emerges from the Swan River Valley into a congested but charming area signaling your arrival in the Flathead. Bigfork is one of Montana's favorite destination playgrounds, especially in the summer. Its picturesque setting where the river dumps into placid Flathead Lake bay has become a draw for money and the quaint shops, high-end restaurants with creative chefs, galleries, live theater, marina, golf, and related activities that come with it. Bigfork has envisioned this persona for itself since 1937, when a major fire gutted the Bigfork Hotel and allowed the town's fathers to rethink its future. The result was an 18-room Swiss chalet–style hotel reminiscent of Glacier National Park's lodging; it was renamed the **Bigfork Inn**, and it became a magnet for the rich, the famous, and others passing through.

Plan to spend a day in Bigfork. Rent a bike or kayak, book a charterboat or sailboat cruise, look for birds and wildflowers along the "Wild Mile" **Swan River Nature Trail**, play 18 holes at **Eagle Bend Golf Club**, take in a show at the **Bigfork Summer Playhouse**, roll out a blanket for the Sunday evening **River Bend Concert Series** at Sliter Park, picnic at **Wayfarers State Park** just south of town. Or simply wander amid the shops on Electric Avenue—named for the town's most prominent feature, a century-old hydroelectric dam on the Swan River. There is a wide assortment of lodging and dining from which to choose.

Joshua Wetsit's teepee in the Pioneer Museum of Valley County, in Glasgow, is believed to be one of three left in the world made of buffalo hide.

CHAPTER

9

Montana's Endless Horizon: The Hi-Line

Glasgow to Shelby

Estimated length: 260 miles
Estimated time: 5 hours to 3 days

Highlights: Dinosaur trail museums and field stations, Sleeping Buffalo Hot Springs, Sleeping Buffalo Rock, Bowdoin National Wildlife Refuge, Blaine County Wildlife Museum, Bear Paw Battlefield, Havre Beneath the Streets, Havre Railroad Museum, Fort Assinniboine, H. Earl Clack Museum, Wahkpa Chu'gn Buffalo Jump, Marias Museum of History & Art.

Getting there: We recommend starting your Hi-Line adventure in Glasgow, in part because you will end up at Glacier National Park's doorstep. You can include the Big Sky Backcountry Byway tour by leaving I-94 at Terry and continuing north to Wolf Point on MT 263, MT 200, and MT 13. From Wolf Point, it's 47 miles west on US 2 to Glasgow. The west end of the Hi-Line is accessed by taking I-15 north at Butte and continuing through Helena and Great Falls to the US 2 East exit at Shelby. In addition, Amtrak parallels US 2 on the busy Burlington Northern Santa Fe route, with twice-daily stops—one each direction—in Glasgow, Malta, Havre, and Shelby. Glasgow is served by Great Lakes Airlines with flights from Wolf Point, Miles City, Billings, and Denver; Havre has Great Lakes flights to and from Lewistown, Billings, and Denver.

Overview

In Montana, where rugged individualism is almost as much a part of the human experience as breathing, even the most leathery residents tip their hats to the weather-toughened residents of the Hi-Line. A hardy constitution is required to carve a life and livelihood out of the wind-sculpted prairies shouldering the turbid Milk River just south of the Canadian border.

This was the last area of Montana to be settled and the first to be deserted. At first glance, there is little here but cattle, barbed wire, and lonely whistle-stop grain elevators to blunt the winds from the north as they roar unchallenged across the prairies from the Arctic and Canada. If it weren't for the distant "island" mountain ranges rising like protective shadows on the horizon, you'd think you'd taken a wrong turn and landed in Nebraska. The reward for residents' fortitude is hot summers amid leafy cottonwood trees in oasis towns 8 to 10 miles apart, lazy days angling for warm-water fish, and evening breezes that may or may not fend off the prodigious mosquitoes. The towns, all but a handful with fewer than 1,000 residents, are some of Montana's loneliest. By the time they sprang up as sidings along the Great Northern Railroad (now Burlington Northern Santa Fe), folks were weary of coming up with new names for western outposts. So most on the Hi-Line were created in an office at the Great Northern headquarters in Minneapolis, where a railroad employee was blindfolded, a globe spun, and a finger randomly aimed. The result was such incongruous post office addresses as Glasgow and Inverness (Scotland), Zurich (Switzerland), Malta (island in the Mediterranean Sea), Saco (Maine), Hinsdale (Illinois), Harlem (New York), and Joplin (Missouri). Folks in Chinook did localize theirs—they named their comfortable little town for the winter winds that blow off the Rockies with such ferocity that a minus 20-degree day can turn to plus-30 degrees in a few hours, or vice versa.

The Hi-Line is so-called because the railroad and then US 2 cut a gradually rising straight east–west line that begins at the North Dakota border and slams into the Rocky Mountains about 450 miles later. It came to be in the 1890s, when the discovery of Marias Pass between present-day Glacier National Park and the Bob Marshall Wilderness enabled James J. Hill to push his Great Northern Railroad from Minot, North Dakota, across Montana's northern tier. As one of the few regions of Montana where towns are actually shrinking, spending a day strolling Main Street along the Hi-Line is like stepping into a Rockwell painting. Rusting farm imple-

Hinsdale's Hi-Line pride is reflected in a mural along US 2.

ments, battered grain elevators with flocks of pigeons, and the whistle of frequent trains provide much of its character.

Even the Hi-Line's contemporary tourism marketing is tied to a very distant past—many of the museum stops on the Montana Dinosaur Trail are located here. This area has produced some of the world's greatest dinosaur finds, and many are on display. Most of the museums, dinosaur or otherwise, typically are only open in the summers—though managers will give private tours if you twist their arms.

To know the Hi-Line is to take your time exploring it. The 260 miles from Glasgow to Shelby can easily be driven in five hours, but treat yourself to a slower pace. Take a closer look with each passing mile, and you'll begin to see the subtle differences in landscapes and people with more personality than meets the eye.

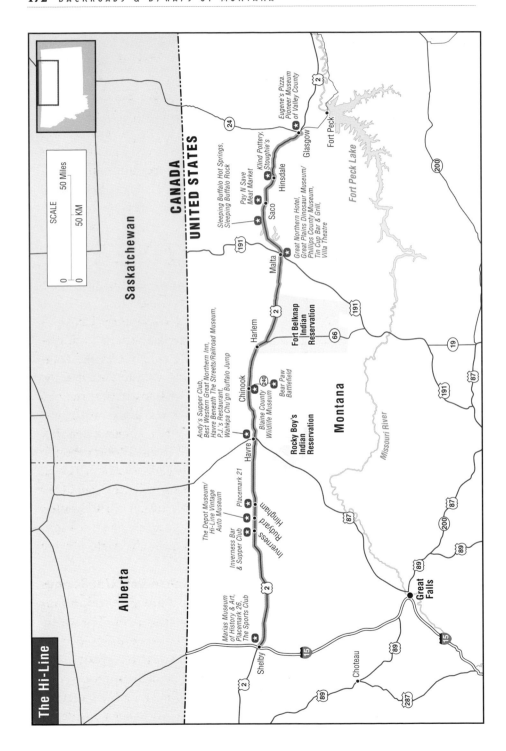

The Hi-Line

SCALE

50 Miles

50 KM

Saskatchewan

Alberta

CANADA

UNITED STATES

Montana

Fort Peck Lake

Missouri River

Fort Belknap
Indian
Reservation

Rocky Boy's
Indian
Reservation

Eugene's Pizza,
Pioneer Museum
of Valley County

Fort Peck

Glasgow

Klind Pottery,
Stoughie's

Hinsdale

Sleeping Buffalo Hot Springs,
Sleeping Buffalo Rock

Pay N Save
Meat Market

Saco

Great Northern Hotel,
Great Plains Dinosaur Museum/
Phillips County Museum,
Tin Cup Bar & Grill,
Villa Theatre

Malta

Harlem

Andy's Supper Club,
Best Western Great Northern Inn,
Havre Beneath The Streets/Railroad Museum,
P.J.'s Restaurant,
Wahkpa Chu'gn Buffalo Jump

Chinook

Blaine County
Wildlife Museum

Bear Paw
Battlefield

Havre

The Depot Museum/
Hi-Line Vintage
Auto Museum

Placemark 21

Hingham

Rudyard

Inverness

Inverness Bar
& Supper Club

Marias Museum
of History & Art,
Placemark 26,
The Sports Club

Shelby

Choteau

Great
Falls

Hitting the Road

Glasgow (pop. 3,253) is the starting point for your Hi-Line journey. It's also the gateway to the Fort Peck Dam and Reservoir area covered in the Big Sky Backcountry Byway chapter. Glasgow is unique among Hi-Line towns in that for two decades it had a third major economic influence after agriculture and the railroad: the U.S. Air Force. Glasgow Air Force Base was built during World War II, then shut down in the 1960s. This history is reflected in the fighter jet in the front yard of the **Pioneer Museum of Valley County** (406-228-8692), which has an extraordinary collection of memorabilia ranging from nearly a century of military artifacts to the stories of the area's Indians and homesteaders. The giant teepee just inside the entrance is part of the impressive Joshua Wetsit collection; it purportedly is one of three buffalo-hide teepees left in the world. Any bar in Montana would be thrilled to have the Pioneer Museum's mahogany cherry back bar—bullet hole and all.

Heading northwest out of Glasgow on US 2, look for **Klind Pottery** (406-364-2263) in **Hinsdale** (pop. 609). Gloria Klind has been hand throwing pottery for more than three decades, starting in an old homestead without running water. She attempts to capture the state's wildness in what she calls "Montana's Spirit of the Clay." Klind doubles as postmaster in **Saco** (pop. 225), 14 miles west on US 2. Saco is the the best place on the Hi-Line to stock up with meaty snacks for the journey. For a quarter century, **Pay N Save Grocery and Meat Shop** (406-527-3361) owner Robert Plouffe has been winning awards for his cured meats, especially his ham, bacon, and 20-plus flavors of bratwurst. Saco is unique on at least three other counts: It's the childhood home of the late NBC newscaster Chet Huntley, its school system is nationally recognized for its progressive education, and it owns a natural gas well that provides residents with a virtually free heating source.

About 10 miles west of town on US 2 is **Sleeping Buffalo Hot Springs** (406-527-3370), a developed area that features a 106-degree indoor hot pool, a larger swimming pool with 90-degree waters, and a café. The waters are tinted red from iron oxide—"rust-ic," they call it. It's one of the minerals reputed to have healing powers for local Indians and cowboys. The hot springs are named after **Sleeping Buffalo Rock**, actually two rocks resting under a three-sided shelter at the junction of US 2 and the road to fishing-rich **Nelson Reservoir**. These glacial erratic rocks are considered sacred because they were once mistaken for sleeping bison at a time when herds were scarce. Upon discovering that the sleeping buffalo were rocks, the Indians saw *real* bison in the distance, ensuring food, clothing, and shelter. Now that the rock resides near the highway, carloads of Indians regularly pull alongside and pray before leaving tobacco, colorful flags, coins, and other trinkets as offerings.

After passing the **Bowdoin National Wildlife Refuge** (406-654-2863), a paradise for waterfowl, upland game birds, and big game, you'll arrive in **Malta** (pop. 1,922), a peaceful and shaded hamlet on the Milk River that once was one of the most lawless towns on the frontier. Kid Curry and Butch Cassidy's Wild Bunch made off with $40,000 from a train robbery here. The town has two museums in one—the **Phillips County Museum and H.G Robinson House & Gardens** (406-654-1037) are across a gravel parking lot from the **Great Plains Dinosaur Museum & Field Station** (406-654-5300). A $5 fee will get you into both. The Phillips County Museum focuses on the area's homesteading, Indian, and outlaw history. Part of the Montana Dinosaur Trail, the Great Plains Museum offers more than a glimpse of active archeology with its participatory dig programs and has remarkably preserved dinosaurs that were dug up locally, including either the real mummified Leonardo or a replica—depending on whether the world's most complete dinosaur is at home or on the road. Leonardo is one of four *Brachylophosaurus* in the world and the first largely intact "subadult" dinosaur ever found. If you're in the mood for some traditional entertainment, the **Villa Theatre** (406-654-2750) offers first-run movies—as long as at least five other people have the same idea you do. And in the one-size-fits-all category, **Central Video** (406-654-2161) is the best place in town for movies—not to mention homemade jams, syrups, cookies, and popcorn balls.

About 20 miles west of Malta along the Milk River is the **Fort Belknap Indian Reservation**, created in 1888 as a home for the Gros Ventre and Assiniboine tribes; today, about 5,000 Indians live there. Before arriving in Fort Belknap, just past Three Mile Reservoir, an abandoned pink mission and colorful cemetery will appear on a small hill just north of the highway. Though you can't enter the boarded-up and reputedly haunted **Sacred Heart Mission**, the scene provides a classic photo-op; a respectful walk through the cemetery will reveal native stories to those who listen. Fort Belknap has a small park and clean rest area just off the highway where you can read historic markers about how the Assiniboine tribe split from

Ghosts reputedly haunt the abandoned Sacred Heart Mission on the edge of the Fort Belknap Indian Reservation.

the Yankton Sioux and learn about vision quests on Snake Butte. Leaving the reservation, **Harlem** (pop. 806) has a public picnic area that serves as a memorial to two air force pilots who crashed near here.

Twenty-five miles farther west on the Hi-Line is **Chinook** (pop. 1,386), home of the famous Sugarbeeters high school football team. The skinny smokestack and abandoned factory on the eastern edge of town serve as reminders of futile attempts to raise sugar beets. Wheat is the crop of choice now, but the town clings to a sports team nickname that late-night television host Jay Leno once rated the second strangest in the nation. Sugar-beeter jokes aside, Chinook—originally called Dave's Station—is a sweet place to spend an afternoon (great tennis courts) or even a night. The **Blaine County Wildlife Museum** (406-357-3102, Memorial Day–Labor Day) has five vivid exhibits, including a 25-foot-high diorama of a buffalo jump with four full-sized bison plunging to their deaths in front of two life-sized Indians. The **Blaine County Museum** (406-357-2590, Memorial Day–Labor Day) is clean and polished, with collections ranging from pre-historic times to World War II, a remarkable assortment of books for sale,

A small steel post and tokens mark the site of Chief White Bird's teepee at the Bear Paw Battlefield.

and a multimedia theater where one film explains the tragic 1877 events at the **Bear Paw Battlefield** some 15 miles south on MT 240. It was there, on grassy shoulders above willowy Snake Creek and in the shadows of the Bear's Paw Mountains, where Chief Joseph of the Nez Perce, while surrendering to General Nelson A. Miles after a 1,710-mile journey spanning four months and four states, uttered his famous "I Will Fight No More Forever" speech. A grassy 1-mile interpretive trail offers a haunting look at the events that signified the end of the Indian wars. Engraved inch-high metal posts mark the sites of teepees, including Chief Joseph's, and show where the warriors Ollokot and Looking Glass fell.

Back on US 2, it's 21 miles to **Havre** (pop. 9,390), which will feel positively cosmopolitan with its stoplights, strip malls, chain stores, restaurants, and Montana State University–Northern campus. Originally called Bull-hook Bottoms, the town was built as a trading post not far from Fort Assinniboine. Given that it's at the halfway point between Minneapolis and Seattle, this was to be an important stop on the Great Northern's line, and so Hill asked the town fathers to change Bullhook Bottoms' uncivilized name. They obliged, and because many hailed from France, they called it LeHavre, after a harbor town where the parents of a prominent early home-steader lived. They eventually shortened it to Havre, and a statue of Hill stands in front of the Amtrak station.

Havre is one of many small towns across the West that had two faces: The above-ground face it wanted the rest of the world to see and a sordid below-ground face where gentlemen went to gamble and imbibe, ladies of the evening hung their red lights, and Chinese did laundry and provided opium in a spiderweb of tunnels and open rooms. Where Havre differs is that in 1904 a fire leveled virtually the entire city. Legitimate businesses moved underground, and today history is kept alive at **Havre Beneath the Streets** (406-265-8888). Daily guided tours take visitors past a dentist office, bordello, haunted meat market, livery, drugstore, saloon, Chinese laundry, the wax caricature of booze purveyor Shorty Young in his dank office, and more. Tours start at the **Havre Railroad Museum** (406-265-8888), which is included in the $6 admission. Though focused primarily on the Great Northern, the spacious museum has artifacts from other railroads that opened the West and features a mesmerizing model railroad display.

Six miles southwest of Havre on US 87 are the remnants of **Fort Assinniboine** (406-265-8336/406-265-4000, June–Sept.), where as many as 500 soldiers were stationed on 700,000 acres—the largest military fort west of the Mississippi River. The soldiers presided over north-central Montana and ensured that there would be no trouble from Indians, smugglers, and bootleggers from Canada and that the new settlers could plow the prairie safely. The fort, built as a direct result of the Sioux rout of General Custer at Little Bighorn in 1876 and the flight of the Nez Perce a year later, had more than 100 buildings in its heyday; most were torn down when the fort was ceded to the Rocky Boy's Indian Reservation in 1916. Its most famous res-ident was General John J. "Blackjack" Pershing. Today, a handful of build-ings remain, and daily tours are offered in the summer. To sign up, go to the **H. Earl Clack Memorial Museum** (406-265-4000) in the Holiday Village Shopping Center on Havre's west end. The Clack Museum squeezes a lot into a small space, including a diorama of the Bear Paw battle, dinosaur eggs dating back 75 million years, and artifacts from the **Wahkpa Chu'gn Buffalo Jump** (406-265-6417/406-265-4000, June–Sept.). The buffalo jump seems out of place directly behind the shopping center—or maybe it's the mall that's misplaced. Buffalo jumps are scattered throughout the Northern Rockies, but none is more extraordinary than Wakhpa Chu'gn. Bison bones from 600 to 2,000 years old are stacked 20 feet high precisely as they were discovered in 1961 by a 12-year-old boy named John Brumley. Daily one-hour walking tours ($6) also reveal arrowheads and other artifacts.

West of Havre at the one-blink blur of **Fresno**—where do you suppose the railroad employee's finger landed on the globe on that one?—the Milk River disappears over the horizon to the north behind Fresno Dam. For the next 104 miles to Shelby, while the river spends a few hundred kilometers visiting Canada, the Hi-Line becomes a relatively flat and tree-less string of wheat fields stretching even farther to the horizon than they had from Glasgow to Havre. Six miles up the road from **Hingham** (pop. 157), little **Rudyard** (pop. 596) is home to the best greeting sign on the Hi-Line: "Welcome to Rudyard, Home of 596 Nice People and One Old Sorehead." The "sorehead" is a complete *Gryposaurus* dinosaur discovered nearby, and it's displayed in **The Depot Museum** (406-355-4356, Memorial Day–Labor Day) along with dinosaur trail denizens and homesteading equipment. Down the street is **Hi-Line Vintage Auto Museum** (406-355-4356, Memorial Day–Labor Day), with cars from as far back as 1905.

Shortly after passing through **Inverness** (pop. 103) and virtually vacant **Joplin**, you'll arrive at a small rise in the highway. For miles, the outline of a striking island mountain range has been visible in the distant northwest; those are the Sweet Grass Hills, sacred grounds for the Blackfeet, who believe their creator, Napi, made the range from boulders left over from his work on the Rocky Mountains. Now, as the highway begins a slight southwesterly bend, you'll make out the faint outline of much larger mountains to the west—the Rockies. Soon, **Chester** (pop. 811) will appear in a bowl below, an oasis of trees amid the wheat prairie. Chester features the smallish and neatly kept **Liberty County Museum** (406-759-5256, May–Aug.), with its homesteading history tucked inside a red barn, and the year-round **Liberty Village Arts Center & Gallery** (406-759-5652), which showcases a variety of Montana artists.

The remaining 44 Hi-Line miles to **Shelby** (pop. 3,216) offer a last look at the sweeping prairie as the mountains to the west draw ever closer. The

"Welcome to Shelby" sign is noteworthy for the small sculpted outline of two boxers, a nod to an unforgettable chapter in the town's history. In 1923, Shelby had visions of being the commercial hub of a bustling oil region and all the trappings that come with it. In an effort to shine a spotlight on the fledgling town, city officials convinced heavyweight boxing champion Jack Dempsey to stage a fight there, against Tommy Gibbons. Shelby built a 40,000-seat arena on a farm and acquiesced to every demand made by the iconic champion Dempsey, thinking that revenues from a recent oil strike and ticket sales would ensure financial success. Instead, fewer than 10,000 attended the Fourth of July bout, which Dempsey won in 15 rounds, and Shelby was fleeced by promoter Doc Kearns. Four banks and other businesses went bankrupt trying to cover the $300,000 guarantee, and the town hasn't been the same since. To get a closer look at an event that's still a part of the Shelby psyche, visit the **Marias Museum of History & Art** (406-424-2551, May–Sept.), which has more than 10,000 artifacts. Today, Shelby is a rural stop on I-15, with the obligatory chain motels and restaurants.

Best Places to Bunk

Glasgow: The **Cottonwood Inn & Suites** ($$, 406-228-8213/800-321-8213) has 124 rooms and is the closest to an upscale chain motel in town. The **Campbell Lodge** ($, 406-228-9328) has the look and feel of a 1950s Holiday Inn, and the **Koski Motel** ($, 406-228-2002), adorned in Finlander white and blue, is the choice of those who like quiet, mom-and-pop places.

Saco: **Sleeping Buffalo Hot Springs Resort** ($, 406-527-3370) has four newer motel rooms as well as primitive cabins and other motel rooms.

Malta: The adorable **Maltana Motel** ($$, 406-654-2610), same owners as the Great Northern Hotel, is cheerful and clean.

Chinook: The **Chinook Motor Inn** ($, 406-357-2248) is centrally located with pleasant and reasonable accommodations.

Havre: Most of Havre's motels are located on US 2. The **Best Western Great Northern Inn** ($$, 406-265-4200), **Townhouse Inn of Havre** ($$, 406-442-4667), and **AmericInn** ($$/$$$, 800-634-3444) are some of the more corporate-style, locally recommended places to stay.

Shelby: The **O'Haire Motor Inn** ($/$$, 406-434-5555) downtown is a throwback to the 1950s, when oil and gas execs used it as their base.

Alternative Bunking

Camping: The **Lake Shel-Oole Campground** (406-434-5222) north of Shelby, tucked beneath an earthen dam, has nearly 70 sites for RVs and tents and decent fishing.

Best Eats

Glasgow: Dining options are run-of-the-mill, though **Sam's Supper Club** ($$, 406-228-4614, L/D) has credible steak-and-seafood entrées and some history served with it. The restaurant began as The Club in the 1930s, when the massive Fort Peck Dam was under construction. People from as far away as Malta, Wolf Point, and even Billings—seriously—rave about **Eugene's Pizza** ($/$$, 406-228-8552, D), a community icon for nearly five decades and home of the best broasted chicken around.

Hinsdale: Stoughie's ($/$$, 406-364-2132, B/L/D), a community gathering place complete with a screened front porch, is famed for huge burgers plated with hand-cut french fries, prime rib on Saturdays, homemade soups, and tasty daily specials. Note: Opens at 10 AM for breakfast.

Malta: The **Great Northern Hotel** ($$/$$$, 406-654-2100, B/L/D) restaurant has great biscuits and gravy, broasted chicken, and the locally ubiquitous walleye. In a town not known for its dining options, locals also opt for the **Tin Cup Bar & Grill** ($$, 406-654-5527, B/L/D) because it overlooks the golf course and has decent fare, unique burgers, and the best walleye in Malta. Go with house-made blue cheese for your salad dressing.

Harlem: KB's Deli ($, 406-353-4435, L) has a terrific chicken salad sandwich, chili nachos, and homemade soup; seal the deal with a shake, malted, or ice-cream float.

Chinook: Jean's Old Fashioned Bakery ($, 406-357-4287, B/L) is regionally known for homemade sweets and sandwiches. Get there early for the ooey-gooey caramel rolls.

Havre: Dining options are more diverse than anywhere else on the Hi-Line. Locals head to **Uncle Joe's** ($$/$$$, 406-265-5111, L/D) for super-sized steaks, the onion blossom, and broasted chicken. **P.J.'s Restaurant & Casino** ($$, 406-265-3211, B/L/D) is the place for prime rib or smoked baby back ribs, and there's **Andy's Supper Club** ($$/$$$, 406-265-9963, D) for platter-sized steaks and Alaskan king crab; plan on leftovers. You can get a Gaelic Boxty (a potato pancake layered with beef sirloin, onions, and mushrooms and covered with Irish whiskey cream sauce) and micro-brew at **Murphy's Irish Pub** ($/$$, 406-265-4700, L/D). For the obvious and not-so-obvious meatball sandwich or chicken and spinach cannel-loni, all prepared with caring hands, it's **Nalivka's Original Pizza Kitchen** ($/$$, 406-265-4050, L/D).

Hingham: At **Hi-Way Bar & Quick Stop** ($, 406-397-3266, L/D) you can treat yourself to inexpensive, good eats while marveling at your luck for finding such a bargain in the middle of seemingly nowhere.

Inverness: The **Inverness Bar & Supper Club** ($/$$, 406-292-3801, L/D) lures diners from as far as Great Falls and Havre for reasonably priced steaks, supreme walleye, and an "X-rated" drink made of vodka, mango, passion fruit, and grapefruit.

Chester: The **Grand Bar & Grill** ($/$$, 406-759-5582, D) once was called the Chic N Coop because of its broasted chicken, still their best seller. You will also find seafood, steaks, burgers (with homemade fries), and top-notch salads (steak, grilled chicken, taco). Prime rib on Saturday nights ($19) is a worthy splurge. Weekends are crowded, as is Monday during football season.

Dunkirk: The **Frontier Bar & Supper Club** ($$$, 406-432-3600, D) is 10 miles east of Shelby, and though it serves huge steaks with the usual sides, it's also the best place for seafood: salmon, halibut, mussels, and oyster shooters served in a shot glass with vodka—slurpin' good.

Shelby: The **Sports Club** ($$, 406-424-8100, L/D) is a "different kind of place…sort of," according to owners Karen and Matt, both native Mon-tanans. They bring a whisk of gourmet to standard cuisine with their smokehouse burger (cheddar cheese, BBQ sauce, and onion rings), sweet potato fries (a first in Shelby), creative salads (Thai chicken), soups (spicy peanut), and fried cheesecake (indecent decadence).

Best Bars

Hingham: The **Hi-Way Bar & Quick Stop** (406-397-3211) is a respite from sore-butt syndrome, and appeals to families, bikers, and John Deere drivers alike. Sit a spell, chill with a beverage, and load up on good eats for less than $10. Where else but in Hingham can you find a burger special (Wednesday nights) for $2.50? Add a side of fries ($2) and a cold brew, and your tab is still less than a ten-spot, tip included. Other popular dinner specials are the broasted chicken (Mondays and Fridays) that comes with four pieces, salad, and glorified french fries called jojos for a mere $8.25. The husband-and-wife team of Mike and Kylie, with an assist from friend Spencer, has a good thing going: She runs the kitchen while he works the front end. Lunch is blue-plate style, and although limited in selection, is not short on tastiness. And there's talk of a cook-your-own-steak night. You'll especially enjoy the conversations if you're a Minnesota Vikings fan.

Inverness: Boots, buckles, and cowboy hats mixed with scrubbed and shining ladies balance well in the **Inverness Bar & Supper Club** (406-292-3801). On the bar side, it's comfortably cramped, with slightly dusty dark wood, functional back bar, and faded turquoise barstools. Around the corner is the dining side with tables dressed in grayish blue and white. The buzz is as genuinely congenial as the servers. The place has been in the Dahlke family for 50 years; daughter Shawn and her husband Elton have had it since the late 1990s. The bar has entertainment that crosses generational lines: big-screen, gaming machines, foosball table, and darts. Also friendly are the prices: A burger will run you less than $4, and the supper club is popular for its walleye, fried shrimp, and the "keep 'em coming back" steaks. Try the steamed cod served with drawn butter and a salad topped with house-made blue-cheese dressing.

The Perfect Weekend

Even though you can drive the entire Hi-Line in five or six hours, doing it justice will require a three-day weekend. Start by visiting the **Pioneer Museum of Valley County** and then find out why people drive from miles around for **Eugene's Pizza** in Glasgow. Spend the night at the **Cotton-wood Inn & Suites** and rise for a late breakfast at **Stoughie's** in Hinsdale before visiting **Klind Pottery**. After breakfast, pick up some jerky, sausage, and other lunch-on-the-go foods at the **Pay N Save Groceries & Meat Market** in Saco. After stopping for a quiet moment at **Sleeping Buffalo Rock**, turn north for an early-afternoon soak and picnic lunch at **Sleeping Buffalo Hot Springs**. Drive into Malta and check into the **Maltana Motel**

Underground frontier history comes to life at Havre Beneath the Streets.

before or after visiting the **Great Plains Dinosaur Museum** and **Phillips County Museum**. Have dinner overlooking the golf course at the **Tin Cup Bar & Grill** before taking in a movie at the **Villa Theatre**. When morning rolls around, have breakfast at the **Great Northern Hotel** before pointing west. Veer off US 2 at the **Fort Belknap Indian Reservation** to learn about vision quests before continuing on a midday tour of the **Bear Paw Battlefield** south of Chinook. Back in Sugarbeeter land, see life-size bison and Indians at a buffalo jump diorama at the **Blaine County Wildlife Museum**. Continue into Havre for a late lunch at **Uncle Joe's** and an afternoon tour of **Havre Beneath the Streets** and the **Havre Railroad Museum**. Check into the **Best Western Great Northern Inn** before having a late dinner at

STEP *WAY* BACK IN TIME ON THE MONTANA DINOSAUR TRAIL

Human history has its Olduvai Gorge. Dinosaur history has its Montana. And it all comes into sharp focus on the 15-stop Montana Dinosaur Trail, which includes five museums and field stations on the Hi-Line.

Dinosaurs once roamed the entire earth, but few places combine the necessary ingredients for discoveries like Montana. The state still has open spaces and boasts a wide variety of exposed rocks from every geologic era in the planet's history. The result is a potpourri of dinosaur types—from the land, air, and even a sea that once covered parts of the state.

The *Guinness Book of World Records* calls Malta's Leonardo, a mummified *Brachylophosaurus,* the best-preserved dinosaur anywhere. The first, largest, and one of the most complete *Tyrannosaurus rex* fossils in the world have all been unearthed here and now reside at Fort Peck. A duckbill dinosaur's eggs from the ancient Bearpaw Sea are on display on the H. Earl Clack Museum in Havre. The motherly *Maiasaura* is Montana's state fossil.

In all, the preserved remains of at least 25 types of dinosaurs have been found across the state, and their actual fossils or replicas are the centerpiece of museums in the tiniest of towns. The Dinosaur Field Station in Malta, Fort Peck Field Station of Paleontology, Garfield County Museum in Jordan, Two Medicine Dinosaur Center in Bynum, and Makoshika Dinosaur Museum in Glendive all offer the opportunity to get your hands dusty on guided field digs.

The Montana Dinosaur Trail is a marketing effort by the state to attract tourists to places that don't see many visitors and often struggle economically. But the exhibits are impressive and the concept isn't gimmicky, other than perhaps the Montana Dinosaur Trail "passport" in which stamps from all 15 sites results in a free T-shirt.

Andy's Supper Club. On the way out of Havre in the morning, grab breakfast at **P.J.'s Restaurant** and then marvel at the piles of ancient bones at the **Wahkpa Chu'gn Buffalo Jump.** Settle in for the short drive to Hingham and talk Vikings football during lunch at the **Hi-Way Bar & Quick Stop.** After that, take your time visiting the "Old Sorehead" in **The Depot Museum** and gawk at the classic cars in the **Hi-Line Vintage Auto Museum,** both in Rudyard. Be sure to stop either for an afternoon beverage or dinner at the **Inverness Bar & Supper Club.** If time permits, you'll want to tour the **Marias Museum of History & Art** in Shelby, especially for the exhibits about the ill-fated Dempsey-Gibbons boxing match in 1923. Still hungry?

The **Sports Club** in Shelby offers fine fare to close a long day, and you'll have a lengthy list of motels to choose from, including the iconic **O'Haire Motor Inn**.

DETOUR: ONE FOR THE ROAD

The Missouri Breaks

Winifred to Charles M. Russell National Wildlife Refuge

Estimated length: 92 miles

Highlights: Missouri Breaks, Charles M. Russell National Wildlife Refuge, Winifred Museum, McClelland Ferry, Woodhawk Trail.

Getting there: From the south, each route that leads to the byway starts at Big Timber—Exit 367 if you're coming from the west, 370 from the east. Drive north on US 191 through Harlowton and Lewistown to Hilger. Here you'll have to decide between taking County Road 236 directly north 23 miles to Winifred or continue on US 191 to just before the Missouri River. Looking west on Knox Ridge Road you'll quickly be able to tell whether the dirt road is navigable; it can be extremely soupy here after a rainstorm.

It doesn't take much imagination to contemplate bygone eras on the snow-white coulees of the **Missouri Breaks**. After all, little has changed in the two centuries since Lewis and Clark arrived at these forbidding badlands, and barely a century has passed since the flight of the Nez Perce ended a few miles to the north. The modern world doesn't spend much time here, except in canoes, kayaks, and rafts plying the lazy waters of the **Wild and Scenic Missouri River** and the occasional pickup kicking up dust on the **Charles M. Russell National Wildlife Refuge**. In a state renowned for its solitude, ruggedness, and raw beauty, the Missouri Breaks has few peers.

First, a warning: The entire route might not be navigable, even in July or August. A good rainstorm can turn parts of the road to gumbo, and even if you have a high-clearance and/or four-wheel-drive vehicle, you could wind up stuck a long way from anywhere. The closest town of any size is **Lewistown** (pop. 5,813), 37 miles from the route's hub in **Winifred** (pop. 156). If the weather has been rainy or threatening, save your trip for another day. If negotiable, however, this route provides a marvelous glimpse of the famed White Cliffs of the Missouri and vast grasslands of both the wildlife refuge and the **Upper Missouri River Breaks National Monument**.

The drive has earned a Backcountry Byway designation in part because of its historical significance: Lewis and Clark camped here in 1805 and dubbed it "The Deserts of America." The Nez Perce came through on their unsuccessful flight to Canada in 1877. Appreciation of a stark natural world is a must. There are no services along the route except at Winifred, a bright agricultural town with an extraordinary little museum.

The Missouri River is most responsible for this spectacular rock sculptures in the White Cliffs and badlands areas. For it was the river that cut through alternating soft shale and hard sandstone, allowing for an array of tall, thin, and eerie rock features called hoodoos and pedestal rocks that look like toadstools. Montanans have an abiding affection for this arid area, and a journey in a river craft is a popular pastime.

Though the Missouri Breaks Backcountry Byway can be reached from US 191, begin your trip in Winifred. A classic prairie town, Winifred is the proud and tight-knit gateway to the region and a necessary stop to appreciate local history and culture. The **Winifred Museum** has the requisite assortment of historical homesteader, Indian, and dinosaur artifacts, but the primary reason to stop here is for what the town claims—and after seeing it, who's to doubt?—to be the largest collection of Tonka trucks anywhere. The museum is open only in summers, but if you're there during the off-season give them a call and they'll gladly come by and open up.

Winifred is also the only place on the route to grab a bite to eat, either at the **Winifred Tavern & Cafe** or **Trails Inn Bar**—both of which serve what you'd expect in rural Montana—and you can gas up at the Cenex. In 2010, the historic building that houses the **Winifred Grocery** was being renovated with an eye on retaining its old character.

As you drive about a mile east from Winifred on Knox Ridge Road to begin the byway, go off the beaten byway about 12 miles to the free **McClelland Ferry**, one of three left crossing the Missouri. The McClelland Ferry, also called the Stafford Ferry, is nearly a century old. Make the detour just to experience a vanishing piece of frontier history and talk to the operators of the diesel-powered craft.

Back at the junction near Winifred, head east again and drive another 11 miles to the next junction: Two Calf Road. Here begins the byway loop. The more improved Knox Ridge Road continues to the east; the more scenic but slower Two Calf Road route goes north and eventually reaches the rim above the Missouri. If you're feeling especially adventurous, take some of the two-track trails veering off toward the rim for some spectacular views of the river, distant mountains, and geology peeled away an era at a time in the cliffs. Fourteen miles into Two Calf Road is the **Woodhawk Trail**, which leads to a dramatic overlook. Continue another 2 miles on Two Calf Road, and you'll reach Woodhawk Bottoms Road, which leads down to the river. Two miles beyond Woodhawk Bottoms Road is Power Plant Ferry Road—this one to the site of an old ferry, the only crossing in the area until Fred Robinson Bridge on US 191 was built. And that isn't the last road to the Missouri: Five miles beyond Power Plant Ferry Road is 2-mile-long Heller Bottom Road, which might be the most scenic of the bunch.

About 30 miles into the northern route is the western end of the 125-mile-long, 1.1-million-acre **Charles M. Russell National Wildlife Refuge,** a small portion of which is west of US 191. The refuge was created in 1936 to preserve habitat for the pronghorn and sharp-tail groused. Some 60 mammals and 220 bird species are here year-round, and if conservationists have their way, there'll be one more mammal—the bison.

The byway loop roads reconnect about 5 miles west of US 191. The return 23-mile trip across sage plains will surely be quicker, but take your time—even though you're away from the river there's still plenty of wildlife to see.

Pronghorn, also commonly called antelope, look for winter forage in the Terry Badlands.

CHAPTER

10

The Big Open: Big Sky Backcountry Byway

Terry to Wolf Point

Estimated length: 105 miles
Estimated time: 3 hours to 2 days

Highlights: Terry Badlands, Cameron Gallery, Prairie County Museum, McCone County Museum, Fort Peck Dam Interpretive Center and Museum, Kempton Hotel.

Getting there: Veer off I-90 a few miles east of Billings onto I-94. Take Exit 176 from I-94 at Terry. On the northernmost point, Wolf Point is on US 2 and the Amtrak line, and it is served by Big Sky Airlines as well. The closest major regional airports are in Billings, 175 miles to the southwest of Wolf Point, and Williston, North Dakota, 130 miles to the northeast.

Overview

Some call it the Big Open. Some call it the Big Dry. Others think of it simply as the forgotten Montana. Whatever it's called, the Big Sky Backcountry Byway is a memorable experience as much for what it once was—and could be again—as it is for what little there is to see and do in this vast country that's largely devoid of humans and their trappings.

With only the slightest imagination, you can gaze from the windows of your car and envision bison outlined against amber hillsides, grazing on tall-grass prairie. Or picture a band of Sioux sitting astride horses above a coulee, scouting for a camp or warily eyeing a wagon train of settlers. Even in our modern world, neither image is overly far-fetched. For it was in the Big Open that the hooves of great bison herds last thundered across Montana, before wanton slaughter in the late 1800s rendered the shaggy beast extinct in this region in all but a remote valley in Wyoming's Yellowstone National Park. And it's here where dreamers see bison roaming this undulating country again as part of a vast national park called the Buffalo Commons. Here also was where the legendary Sioux made a last stand, the most stubborn of the "hostiles" relegated to the arid and inhospitable Fort Peck Indian Reservation north of the Missouri River. At a forgotten place called Cedar Creek, about 35 miles north of Terry, the Sioux chief Sitting Bull—best known for orchestrating Custer's demise at Little Bighorn—surrendered to General Nelson A. Miles in the autumn of 1876, permanently returning to the rez. The Indians were treated nearly as shabbily as the bison, and similarly what remains of a shattered culture today bears little resemblance to yesteryear.

This is some of the country that inspired great western writers. It also was the inspiration for Montana's best-known name outside the state: Big Sky Country. The byway bisects the Big Open from south to north—through McCone and Prairie counties, from Terry on the meandering Yellowstone to Wolf Point on the mighty Missouri. It's part of an old trade route connecting Regina, Saskatchewan, with Yellowstone. Lonely windmills seem to outnumber lonelier trees, and you're as likely to see a pronghorn or mule deer as a cow or horse—or human. All of 2,000 people live in McCone County, which covers 1.7 million acres. In the 105 miles between Wolf Point and Terry are two towns: Circle and Brockway, once thriving cattle towns now clinging to an image in a region rapidly losing its youth to larger towns. Cattle and sheep outnumber humans about 100 to one in rugged country where the annual rainfall is only slightly higher than in Arizona's deserts and winter temperatures of minus-30 degrees aren't an aberration. On the north end of the byway, Wolf Point is a half-Indian, half-white community on US 2 that serves as a regional hub. In these parts, sufficing for a hub is an Albertson's grocery store, a few gas stations, and three serviceable motels.

If you're wanting to be wowed, you've come to the wrong place. The beauty here is stark, subtle, and nuanced. There are no towering mountains, no glistening rivers, no thick forests rich with wildlife, no scenic vistas. Stop and listen to the silence, ruffled only by the whisper of breezes massaging the sagebrush. Stop and look at the hardy flora and fauna in small coulees in the Terry Badlands. Or just sit and admire a fiery sunset that seems to go from here to eternity, and then marvel at the night lighting up with more stars than you'd ever imagine—all seemingly close enough to pluck from the sky. This is Big Sky Country.

Hitting the Road

Chances are your adventure will start in **Terry** (pop. 611), a blip on I-94 between Miles City and Glendive. About one-third of vast Prairie County's residents live here. The town, named for a general who was instrumental in winning the Indian wars, is largely built around agriculture, though it becomes noticeably more crowded during hunting seasons in the fall. Terry's arrival is previewed by the sight of the barren, erosion-pocked hills rising immediately to the north of town above the Yellowstone River. These are the **Terry Badlands** (406-233-2800), and if you appreciate unusual geologic formations sculpted by years of wind, rain, and heat, you'll want to spend a day exploring here.

Before heading into the badlands, though, there is at least one mandatory stop in Terry: The **Cameron Gallery** (406-635-4966). Lady Evelyn Cameron was a strong-willed British woman who moved to the Wild West to homestead in the late 1800s, including a year in Prairie County. She

Pioneer photographer Evelyn Cameron's photos are showcased at the Cameron Gallery in Terry.

brought a camera and began capturing the unvarnished black-and-white essence of prairie life in eastern Montana. Though Cameron's keen eye generated some fame in her new home and some back in England, her compelling photos weren't brought to full life until the 1970s, when boxes full of negatives were found in the basement of a friend's home—nearly a half century after she died. Soon after, the book *Photographing Montana 1894–1928: The Life and Work of Evelyn Cameron* was published, and today her riveting photos are on display in the Cameron Gallery.

For others who are history minded, the **Prairie County Museum** (406-635-4040) next door is full of the type of homesteading equipment Cameron was so adept at capturing on film. The museum also reflects the town's connection to the Northern Pacific Railroad and offers memorabilia you'll surely see nowhere else—a steam-heated outhouse. The museum is in an old stone bank building next to the Cameron Gallery and is open every day except Tuesday from Memorial Day Weekend through Labor Day Weekend. After lunch or breakfast, peruse the new byway kiosk at the 4 Corners gas station before crossing the Yellowstone River on MT 253 and rising into the white, scoria-capped buttes of the badlands.

The Terry Badlands is a federal wilderness study area overseen by the Bureau of Land Management, meaning the government has deemed the area wild and scenic enough to consider including it in the 1964 Wilderness Act. Until that happens, the spires, natural bridges, and other extraordinary landforms in the 45,000-acre area are accessible by motor vehicle. The best access is a left turn off MT 253 three miles north of Terry, though an unimproved road enters from the west on an abandoned railroad grade. This is rugged travel on dirt, and the primitive roads turn to tire-grabbing muck on rare rainy days. It's a Mecca for rock hounds and fossil enthusiasts, and there is a rainbow of vivid colors on sandstone hoodoos and prairie potholes. Translucent agates of varying shapes and colors are found in the badlands and along the Yellowstone, many destined to be honed into jewelry with a diamond saw.

If you aren't inclined to hike in the badlands, you have the option of taking a popular drive out to **Scenic Vista**, where a kiosk explains what you're seeing. Three miles north of Terry, turn left on Scenic View Road. After a short time, you'll come to a cattle grate and gate installed in 2009 by the owner of the property the road crosses. As of early 2011, the state of Montana and the landowner were working to resolve a dispute and ensure public access to an overlook tourists have been visiting unimpeded for 45 years.

Out of the badlands, MT 253 rises gently over the Big Sheep Mountains, molehills by Montana standards. The Big Sheep represent the continental divide between the Yellowstone and Missouri, which eventually meet about 80 miles away on the Montana–North Dakota border. To the west is Big Sheep Mountain, a 3,625-foot bump that's the range's apex. Aside from an occasional distant ranch and windmill, there is little sign of activity until the town of **Brockway** (pop. 140), at the junction of MT 253 and 200. You'd never guess it from its weary facade, but Brockway was the country's number-one livestock shipping port in 1934 and even featured a drive-in movie theater as recently as 1962. Northern Pacific Railroad cars arrived empty and left full of livestock and wheat, barley, and hay. Look closely amid the weeds, and you'll see the abandoned old railroad grade, a microcosm of a town that says it's "proud of its past and optimistic about its future" as it celebrated its centennial in 2010. On the third Saturday each July, the town returns to its robust roots with the **Brockway Dairy Days Rodeo** (406-485-2543), which began in 1918 and boasts no fewer than 21 cowboys and cowgirls who eventually participated in the National Finals Rodeo in Las Vegas.

Turn right on MT 200 and venture another 10 miles along the nondescript Redwater River into the agricultural community of **Circle** (pop. 584), another town that clearly has seen more robust days. Arriving from the south, you'll see the **McCone County Museum** (406-485-2414, May–Oct.) on the right. Inside are more than 7,000 historical items, including more than 200 mounted animals and birds that call the Big Open home. In recent years, a Northern Pacific Railroad depot and caboose, homestead, church, and prairie school have been moved to the grounds. You'll also notice a statue of a *Brontosaurus* in town, a nod to the many fossilized dinosaur bones found in the area. If the creatures that roamed what had been swamps 65 million years ago pique your interest, take a side trip from Brockway about 70 miles west to Jordan on MT 200. Aside from being known as the most remote county seat in the nation and the site of a standoff between the FBI and a group called the Freemen in 1996, Jordan is also dinosaur central in Montana. A virtually complete *Tyrannosaurus rex* skeleton was discovered here in the late 1990s and has since been moved to the Museum of the Rockies in Bozeman.

Circle, named for the brand on a nearby ranch, has several gas stations, all offering diesel. The town also has the only two cafés between Terry and Wolf Point. At the north end of town continue straight on MT 13, toward Wolf Point.

The only community between Circle and Wolf Point is the unincorporated **Vida** (pop. 70), which has two churches, a post office, and a dance hall. By this point, you might feel as if you've been transported from Big Sky Country into central Nebraska. The land is flatter, and distant grain elevators are visible in both directions along US 2. **Wolf Point** (pop. 2,663) is the largest town on the byway and has long served as an Indian trading post on the north bank of the Missouri. Long gone are the days when wolves were common here. Reviled by the European culture, wolves were hunted and trapped relentlessly, and their hides were stacked here waiting for steamboats to take them for sale in the Midwest and East. Wolves were eradicated by the 1880s, but the name remains. When the **Fort Peck Indian Reservation** was created in 1912, with Wolf Point as its largest town, the buildings were moved away from the river to the Northern Pacific line.

If you happen to be in Wolf Point the second weekend in July, the **Wild Horse Stampede** (406-653-2012) is Montana's oldest rodeo. For year-round visitors, the town is hoping to break ground soon just off US 2 on a sprawling **Montana Cowboy Hall of Fame & Western Heritage Center** (406-653-3800), whose mission is to celebrate both the region's frontier and Indian cultures. An opening date remained uncertain in 2011; until then, the center has a temporary site on Third Avenue in Wolf Point. Legacy inductees already include Sitting Bull, Evelyn Cameron, C. M. Russell, and Chief Plenty Coups.

For a side trip, 22 miles east of Wolf Point on US 2 is **Poplar** (pop. 911), hardscrabble tribal headquarters for the Sioux and Assiniboine tribes. The two are culturally similar, but the Assiniboine don't think of themselves as Sioux. They live west of Tule Creek on the reservation, while the Sioux live to the east. For a revealing portrait of life on the reservation, spend $1 on a copy of the weekly *Fort Peck Journal* (see sidebar).

Perhaps the most interesting human-created attraction in the area is the **Fort Peck Dam**, 35 miles west of Wolf Point—reached either by taking US 2 on the north side of the Missouri or the more interesting County Road 528 to MT 24 on the south side. Start your visit at the **Fort Peck Dam Interpretive Center and Museum** (406-526-3493) between the huge dam's powerhouses and campgrounds. Built over seven years at the height of the Great Depression (1933–40), Fort Peck is one of the world's largest earthen dams and employed more than 11,000 workers at the height of construction, turning quiet villages into 18 raucous Wild West boomtowns overnight. As many as 50,000 people lived here at the height of the project. The numbers for the nation's fifth-largest man-made lake are staggering: a dame 21,000 feet long and 250 feet high, 1,520 miles of shoreline, a lake 134 miles long, 18.7-million-acre-feet of water, and a drainage area of 10,200 square miles. The interpretive center explains the magnitude of this endeavor in photos and journals. Also on display are dinosaur bones unearthed during the construction, including yet another skeleton of a *Tyrannosaurus rex*. Fort Peck Reservoir, surrounded by the **Charles M. Rus-**

sell National Wildlife Refuge (406-538-8706), has become a recreation hub for boaters, fishermen, and hunters. If you want to see this area at its wildest—it's the fourth-most visited place in Montana—come in early July for the **Montana Governor's Cup Walleye Tournament** on Fort Peck Reservoir. More than 50 types of fish swim the waters of Fort Peck, but there's little question that the walleye ranks number 1, as evidenced by the hundreds of anglers lured from around the country and Canada for the tournament. While visiting the Fort Peck area in the summer, plan an evening at the ornate **Fort Peck Summer Theatre** (406-526-9943), which has been graced by the likes of Will Rogers, Joan Crawford, William Powell, Shirley Temple, and, to this day, Floyd the Friendly Ghost. Shows, which run Memorial Day Weekend through Labor Day Weekend, have included *Annie* and *The Will Rogers Follies* in summer 2010.

Unlike the Terry Badlands and other points along the Big Sky Backcountry Byway, Fort Peck will test your ability to imagine what it was like before the Euro invasion. Long gone are the days when the Sioux and Assiniboine hunted the cottonwood bottoms along a free-flowing Missouri. Yet even here, what was once unimaginable might soon become reality. Both the Fort Peck Indian Reservation and the rugged white cliffs of the Charles M. Russell National Wildlife Refuge around the reservoir might one day be thundering again under the hooves of wild Yellowstone National-al Park bison, returning a slice of long-lost history and restoring a frontier spirit to the Big Open.

BONNIE RED ELK'S LITTLE NEWSPAPER THAT COULD

To best understand the ongoing Third World triumphs and tragedies of the modern-day Plains Indians on six of Montana's seven reservations, pick up a copy of the *Fort Peck Journal*—one of the few independently operated Indian publications in the country.

The *Journal* is produced in a tiny building in Poplar that looks like a detached garage, but what comes out of there every week under the guidance of a diminutive Sioux woman named Bonnie Red Elk is nothing short of extraordinary. In an era where newspaper circulation is hemorrhaging, the *Journal* is an anomaly. People on and off the Fort Peck Indian Reservation queue up every Thursday, waiting for a copy of a black-and-white tabloid that looks like something from the 1950s. After all, if it happens on the rez, the Sioux and Assiniboine who share the lands know it'll be in the *Journal*—warts and all, unvarnished and unbiased.

Red Elk took over the tribal paper, the *Wotanin,* in the mid-1970s and immediately turned a glorified newsletter into a real newspaper. Her diligence in reporting tribal issues and finances endeared her with the people and infuriated some of the leaders. Eventually, her dogged pursuit of how the tribal chairman used funds for personal travel got her fired from the *Wotanin;* a few weeks later, she started the independent *Journal* on her kitchen table, using a home computer, a

Bonnie Red Elk runs her courageous, independent tribal newspaper in a tiny building in Poplar.

printer, and glue sticks. Readers and advertisers from the *Wotanin* quickly shifted to the *Journal,* and before long, the *Wotanin* was out of business.

The *Journal* is available every Thursday afternoon in each community on the reservation along US 2, from Culbertson to Nashua.

Best Places to Bunk

Terry: There are no traditional or chain motels in town; those are 38 miles to the southwest in Miles City or 40 miles to the northeast in Glendive, both on I-94. Terry's most notable lodging offering is the **Kempton Hotel** ($, 406-635-5543), built in 1912 and the oldest continually operating hotel in Montana. Calamity Jane and former president Theodore Roosevelt are among its more celebrated guests. The Kempton has an adjacent antique shop and does exude a certain charm, but luxurious it isn't—at least until the new owners begin a planned remodel. Rooms are available by the night, and cabins out back are rented by the week or longer for hunters or residents. The **Diamond Motel & Campground** ($, 406-635-5407) is a motor-court operation just down the street.

Circle: Circle's one motel, **The Traveler's Inn** ($, 406-485-3323), has 14 serviceable rooms.

Wolf Point: Several comfortable lodging options are available if you want to use the town as a base to explore some of the unique offerings in the surrounding area. The **Homestead Inn** ($, 406-653-1300) and **Big Sky Motel** ($, 406-653-2300) are both on US 2, and the 46-room **Sherman Inn** ($/$$, 406-653-1100) on the edge of old town has a restaurant, lounge, and casino.

Fort Peck: The old **Fort Peck Hotel** ($/$$, 406-526-3266, Apr.–Dec.), which has earned a spot on the National Register of Historic Places, is a stately throwback to the 1930s, when the nearby dam was built and folks swarmed the area. Things are much quieter now, except in the summer and except for the occasional ghost reputedly wandering the creaky halls. Rooms are smallish, with older beds. They don't have televisions, telephones, or, in some cases, showers—hence the modest rates.

Alternative Bunking

Camping: Fort Peck Reservoir has ample camping opportunities, most in appealing locations. If you don't mind having the earthen dam looming over you, **Downstream Camp** (406-526-3411) is set amid leafy cottonwoods and has by far the most amenities. There are 86 sites with electricity, another 13 for tents. Play basketball, walk a milelong nature trail, and turn the kids loose in the play area; you'll likely need advance reservations for this popular campground. The **West End Recreation Area & Campground** (406-526-3411) has 24 sites with views of the lake, including 14 for RVs. Outside Circle you'll find the most intriguing lodging and the best way to fully grasp the subtle rhythms of the region—the **Wolff Farms Vacation Home** ($$/$$$, 406-485-2633). Wolff Farms is a sprawling working farm about 15 miles northwest of Circle, between MT 13 and the massive Fort Peck Reservoir. The rooms are intimate and filled with antiques, and you'll get three hearty meals. But the draw is the wide-open spaces, horseback riding, deer and game-bird hunting, access to fishing and boating on the reservoir, immersion in the prairie way of life, and peace and quiet. They might even let you lasso a calf.

Best Eats

Terry: The cash-only **Dizzy Diner** ($, 406-635-4666, B/L/D) is bright, has wireless Internet, and is a comfortable place to get a burger or chicken strips, fries, shake, and salad. In an area where you're always feeling as if you've stepped back in time, the new **Badlands Cafe & Scoop Shoppe** ($, 406-635-2233, L/D) harkens back to the 1950s. You can't miss it: The hindquarters of a red 1955 Chevy are part of the marquee.

Circle: The **Wooden Nickel Bar & Restaurant** ($, 406-485-2575, L/D) is the only eatery between Terry and Wolf Point. As you might expect in a place surrounded by cattle, the burgers and steaks are locally produced.

Wolf Point: Highlights are the **Old Town Grill** ($, 406-653-1031, B/L/D) and **Wolf Point Cafe** ($, 406-653-1388, B/L/D), both with traditional fare.

Fort Peck: The **Missouri River Grill** ($/$$, 406-526-3266, B/D, Apr.–Dec.) in the Fort Peck Hotel offers an upscale environs unique to these parts. Naturally, one of the local favorites is the walleye, topped with Parmesan cheese and green onions.

Best Bars

Park Grove: Just about every joint says they have the best hamburger in Montana, but the otherwise nondescript **Park Grove Bar & Cafe** (406-526-3252), downstream from the dam, can back it up with a burger deemed best in the state by *Montana Magazine*. That led to the bar's burgers being featured in a "Get Lost in Montana" television commercial. The fresh-ground patties are hand-pressed each day by the DuBeaus. The weathered bar and café, in an old farmhouse set amid the shade of giant cottonwoods, is the only business still operating in the one-time boomtown of Park Grove. The remains of a few abandoned shanties are scattered nearby, relics still clinging to existence eight decades after the heady days of the Great Depression. Another fine bar is the nearby **Gateway**, which dubs itself "The Best Dam Bar by a Dam Site." The Gateway has the usual burger-and-fries bar fare, but is geared toward the younger set.

Perfect Weekend

Chances are you'll be tempted to eat and bunk in Miles City or Glendive before embarking on the Big Sky Backcountry Byway, but we encourage you to fully immerse yourself in this rural experience—a throwback dinner at the **Badlands Cafe & Scoop Shoppe** and lodging at the rustic **Kempton**. After awakening, enjoy some pancakes or eggs at the **Dizzy Diner** before spending the morning marveling at the photos of resilient homesteader Evelyn Cameron at the **Cameron Gallery** and meandering next door to the **Prairie County Museum**. Drive out to the **Scenic Vista** overlooking the **Terry Badlands**. Arrive in Circle in time for a late lunch at **The Wooden Nickel** and visit to the **McCone County Museum**. Continue on through the ranch and farmlands to Wolf Point and secure a room at the **Sherman Inn** before settling in for supper at the **Old Town Grill**. Start your next morning with pancakes at the **Wolf Point Cafe**, take a few hours to explore the **Montana Cowboy Hall of Fame & Western Heritage Center**, and then

Montana Magazine *once dubbed the burgers at Park Grove Bar near Fort Peck the best in the state.*

head out to spend the day at the **Fort Peck Dam Interpretive Center and Museum**. After wandering amid the displays at the dam, see if you agree that the **Park Grove Bar and Café**'s burger really is the best in Montana. If it's summer, make the short drive back to Fort Peck to check into the historic **Fort Peck Hotel**, have a walleye dinner at the **Missouri River Grill**, and take in northeastern Montana's only live performances at the **Fort Peck Summer Theatre**.

DETOUR: ONE FOR THE ROAD

The Prairie

Big Timber to Lewistown

Estimated length: 107 miles

Highlights: Crazy Mountain Museum, Greycliff Prairie Dog Town State Park, Natural Bridge and Falls, Melville Lutheran church, Judith Gap, Gigantic Warm Springs.

Getting there: This rural route starts at one of two exits in Big Timber—Exit 367 from the west and Exit 370 from the east.

Ask longtime residents where they'd choose to live if they could somehow find the perfect blend of scenery, pace, and mix of past and present Montana, and many will whisper "Lewistown." As much as any community in the state, **Lewistown** (pop. 5,813)—with its towering county courthouse rising above leafy streets—embodies a Rockwellian persona.

Lewistown is just close enough to such mountains as the Judith and Big Snowy island ranges to provide a classic modern-day Montana portrait. Yet it's far enough away from the towering ranges and trout streams of glossy magazines to offer isolation and escape the trophy-home frenzy.

The drive from Big Timber to Lewistown doesn't offer much to do. Nor does it have mesmerizing scenery. It's simply mile after mile of eye-pleasing surroundings, with short grasses—that's why they call them Sweet Grass, Wheatland, and Golden Valley counties—swaying against a backdrop of snowcapped mountains in every direction: the burly Absarokas and Beartooths, the deceptively brawny Crazys, the timbered Castles and Little Belts, the captivating Big Snowys, the Judiths standing guard over Lewistown, and, in the shadowy distance, the Highwoods and Little Rockies. Along the way, you'll pass ranches and tractors, white-tailed deer and pronghorn, and get a glimpse of Montana's energy future at Judith Gap, where fields of white wind turbines protrude from the range as far as the eye can see.

The route starts in **Big Timber** (pop. 1,650), home of the Sheepherders and a significant chapter in Lewis and Clark history. Having split with Meriwether Lewis upon the duo's return from the Pacific in 1806, William Clark camped at a spot where the Boulder River and Big Timber Creek joined the Yellowstone River on opposite banks. The creek sported especially large cottonwood trees—hence the name Big Timber. The expedition felled a cottonwood to build a flat-bottomed boat called a *pirogue*. Settled by Norwegians, Big Timber was once one of the last great sheep-ranching areas in Montana. Today, it remains a quiet agricultural community with tree-lined streets, but it's gradually absorbing the spillover of solitude-seeking newcomers from Bozeman and Livingston. The history is encapsulated well at the **Crazy Mountain Museum**, which features a remarkable 1907 replica of the town's 184 buildings. Montanans from as far away as Bozeman and Billings make the drive to Big Timber for dinner at the historic **Grand Hotel**.

Before heading north on US 191, take a few detours from the Detour. The first is a 7-mile drive east on I-90 to **Greycliff Prairie Dog Town State Park**, one of the few places left in Montana where you can see these persecuted critters in all their perky glory. On the way back to Big Timber, another trek to make off the beaten byway is 25 miles south on County Road 298 through **McLeod** (pop. 199), past the farmhouse where scenes from *The Horse Whisperer* were filmed. Continue to the extraordinary **Natural Bridge and Falls** on the Boulder River. The natural arch over the river collapsed in 1988, but the 105-foot falls remain. In lower water, some of the falls disappear and go underground, emerging a short distance downstream. A trail system offers great views of the falls and canyon.

Return the way you came back to Big Timber, take US 191 north for 19 miles to **Melville** (pop. 142), where the state's first Lutheran church was built in 1914 in the foothills of the Crazy Mountains. All but a few of the first services were performed in Norwegian. Beyond Melville, the landscape changes from grass to pine-studded hills off to the right—the sandstone Cayuse Hills. Twenty-five miles north of Melville is **Harlowton** (pop.

Harlowton had one of the great electric railroads in the West.

1,062), another agricultural center. Harlowton was just a small stage stop known as Merino until the Milwaukee Road came along and laid the longest stretch of electric railroad in North America. The state's last electric railway rolled up its tracks in 1974, but its legacy and other area history lives on in the **Upper Musselshell Museum** and in the electric Milwaukee Road railroad car that greets visitors in **Train Park**.

Eighteen miles north of Harlowton on US 191 is **Judith Gap** (pop. 164), named for the gap the Musselshell River creates between the Big Snowy and Little Belt mountains. The gap creates a funnel, and the wind always blows, making the grassy landscape between Harlowton and Judith Gap an ideal place for Montana's first large-scale wind farm. The project went online in 2005, and the 90 turbines rising 262 feet to the big sky produce about 7 percent of the state's electricity.

After passing the wind farm, climb onto an antique tractor seat and enjoy a hand-scooped milkshake at the 1950s-style soda fountain in the **Judith Gap Mercantile**, one of the original buildings in a town founded in 1908. Five miles past Judith Gap is **Garneill**, notable only for a large granite rock that features the names of early pioneers and the dates they arrived in the valley etched in it. The **Ubet and Central Montana Pioneers Monument** sits on a concrete base made of Indian relics, ore, and petrified wood. For the trivia minded, Ubet was a nearby town whose name came from A. R. Barrows, an area resident. When asked if he could figure out what to call the new community, he responded, "You bet!"

In another 14 miles is Eddie's Corner, where you'll turn right at the large gas station at the junction of US 191/89 and MT 200. Drive amid fields of grass toward **Moore** (pop. 186) and another 19 miles to Lewistown. Residents like to think they're the center of Montana's universe—and they're right: Lewistown is at the state's geographic center. It's also unique in that the Judith Basin is home of the all-natural, sparkling-blue Yogo sapphire, the state gem. The sapphires, prized because they are untreated, were found more than a century ago in Yogo Gulch between Utica and Windham west of Lewistown. *Yogo* is the Blackfeet word for "romance," and among the bearers was one Lady Diana Spencer of England, who was presented a nine-carat cornflower-blue sapphire set amid diamonds on a gold ring when Prince Charles asked for her hand in marriage. There's no doubt Lewistown has a love affair with the gem: There's the **Yogo Inn** and **Sapphire Cafe**, among another mineral-inspired names. Local gems for dining include the **Bon Ton Soda Fountain**, a classic 50s-style diner that actually opened in 1908 and fits the town's personality, and **Ruby's 100 Percent Montana Burgers**, famed for all-local beef.

After wandering around Lewistown on a warm summer day, drive 15 miles drive north to cool off in **Gigantic Warm Springs**, one of the largest natural springs in the world. Located on a private ranch, Gigantic Warm Springs produces about 50,000 gallons of water per minute. To call it a warm spring is a stretch—the waters are 68 degrees, ideal on a hot day but not what you'd look for to soothe muscles after a day of cross-country skiing in the Judith Mountains; the fee is $3. After a soak, if it's the weekend, consider closing the day with dinner on wheels aboard the **Charlie Russell Chew Choo**, which rides the old Chicago, Milwaukee, St. Paul, and Pacific rails for 56 miles round-trip from Kingston Junction to Denton. The

$89 fee for adults includes three trestles, a half-mile tunnel, a prime-rib dinner, and possibly a holdup by masked prototypes of Kid Curry, Butch Cassidy, The Sundance Kid, and other notorious gangsters who once roamed this isolated country. The train has nightly departures during the summer as well as on other special occasions during the off-season.

A large, hogan-style structure at Busby lets you know you're in Northern Cheyenne country.

The Warrior Trail:
The Tongue River Loop

Hardin/Crow Agency/Busby/Birney/
Ashland/Lame Deer

Estimated length: 147 miles
Estimated time: 5 hours

Highlights: Little Bighorn Battlefield National Monument, Reno-Benteen Battlefield Memorial, Rosebud Battlefield State Park, Tongue River Reservoir, Wolf Mountains Battlefield National Historic Landmark, St. Labre Mission/Cheyenne Indian Museum, Tongue River.

Getting there: The Warrior Trail begins at the US 212 exit off I-90 (Exit 510) just south of Crow Agency, about 70 miles east of Billings. If you're coming from Billings, consider taking the Detour first: You'll explore some extraordinary country and avoid the monotonous 75-mph hum of the interstate between Billings and Hardin, and you can take a shortcut to the start of the Warrior Trail at Crow Agency.

Overview

No journey through Montana is complete without an immersion in the rich Indian culture that remains today. That experience best comes to life on the Warrior Trail through the Crow and Northern Cheyenne reservations in the south-central part of the state—if you take the time to look. This is not an adventure for the ill prepared or naïve. A large section of the route is on gravel roads—albeit well maintained—through remote country that lacks the services to which Americans are accustomed, even by backroad standards. Life looks and feels decidedly different, and while the tribes are striving to overcome a two-century-old cultural upheaval, the challenges are daunting. Alcoholism, unemployment, and general aimlessness are rampant, and even Indian leaders concede the reservations are reminiscent of Third World cultures. It's readily apparent in the small, colorful, box-shaped, one-size-fits-all homes with the rusting skeletons of old cars in the yards filling the landscape. All the inherent risks of driving rural Montana roads at night—wildlife, alcohol, fatigue—are compounded here.

Yet, there are many more reasons to make this journey than not, starting with the people themselves. You can explore their cultures anytime, but to catch the Crow, Northern Cheyenne, and other Plains Indians in full celebratory regalia, visit during the Crow Fair Powwow in Crow Agency every August. A less boisterous affair is the Northern Cheyenne 4th of July Chief's Powwow & Rodeo in Lame Deer. At Crow Fair, the rolling grasslands in and around Crow Agency become a jovial, sprawling teepee city with thousands of revelers drumming, dancing, and telling tribal stories.

Of course, there's also the Little Bighorn Battlefield National Monument just outside Crow Agency, where the Lakota Sioux and Northern Cheyenne outwitted General George Armstrong Custer and, ironically, his Crow and Arikara scouts in the Indians' most famous military success. The Crow believed if they sided with the U.S. government against the Sioux, Northern Cheyenne, and Nez Perce, they would get to keep much of their vast historic homeland for a reservation. Like every other tribe that signed treaties with Washington, they were sadly mistaken. At 2.3 million acres, their reservation is the largest in Montana, but the Crow lost their prized Stillwater River drainage, the wildlife-rich Paradise Valley, and their sacred Absaroka Mountains.

The Northern Cheyenne Indian Reservation is about one-fifth the size and was born out of desperation. After the Northern and Southern Cheyenne were muted in 1877, they were sent to a reservation in Oklahoma, where the hot and muggy climate was deadly for the unacclimated Northern Cheyenne. When a small band tried to escape, most were killed—but about 125 made it north to Montana and settled near the Tongue River, not far from their traditional homeland in South Dakota's Black Hills. Eventually, the government provided the small reservation that exists today.

Much of the route hugs the Tongue River on the edge of the Northern

The Tongue River forms the eastern edge of the Northern Cheyenne Indian Reservation.

Cheyenne Indian Reservation and traverses rugged prairie, range, and badland country with sharp geological features. Consider bringing a canoe and fishing rod. The meandering Tongue might be Montana's best warm-water stream fishery, with prolific numbers of smallmouth bass, sauger, chub, the prehistoric paddlefish, and the state's sole population of a midwestern fish called the rock bass.

Hitting the Road

For the sake of lodging and dining options, we actually start the Warrior Trail in **Hardin** (pop. 3,384), a mixed agricultural community of Anglos and Indians on the edge of the Crow Reservation.

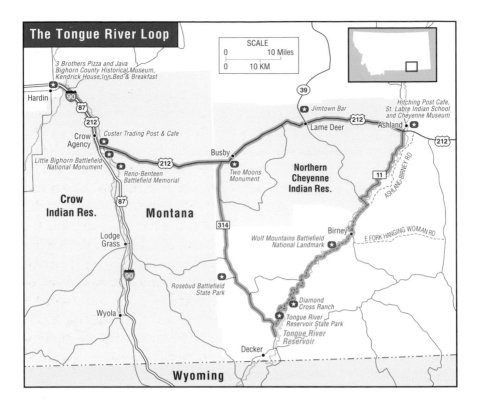

Starting the loop, Hardin is largely nondescript but does have a **Custer's Last Stand Reenactment** in a field northwest of town every June. Some historical buildings are worth seeing, too, including **St. John's Catholic Church** and **Hardin Depot**, but the area's history is best captured at the **Big Horn County Historical Museum & Visitor Center** (406-665-1671). The 22-acre site features more than two dozen outdoor structures and two buildings with exhibits—one focusing on the region's farming traditions, the other on cultural history.

Arriving in **Crow Agency** (pop. 1,552) is not unlike visiting a Mexican border town. The differences between cultures are almost that dramatic, starting with the language. The exit sign reads "Bauxuwuaashee"; weathered buildings featuring similar tongue twisters are interspersed with such newer buildings as those at Little Big Horn College and the Crow/Northern Cheyenne Hospital. When embarking on your journey along the Warrior Trail, which starts at the US 212 exit off I-90, stop at the **Custer Battlefield Trading Post and Cafe** ($, 406-638-2270, B/L/D, shorter hours winter/fall) for a bite and a look at the compelling collection of gifts ranging from the usual jiggers and coffee mugs to fine American Indian art, jewelry, and intricate beadwork. If you're lucky, owner Putt Thompson will be on hand for history lessons. Listen carefully, and you're likely to hear the service staff communicating in Crow. Say "Kay-Ha" (hello), and if they're not busy, ask for the Crow perspective on the nearby **Little Bighorn Battlefield National Monument** (406-638-2621), so named after it was appropriately changed from Custer Battlefield National Monument in 1991. Every American elementary school student knows the story of Custer's Last Stand or, as the Indians call it, the Battle of Greasy Grass Creek. Led by Sitting Bull, the Lakota and Northern Cheyenne overwhelmed Custer and his troops, killing 268 in a battle that galvanized the Anglos against the Indians. The most poignant way to experience the scene is to walk amid the markers where Custer, his 7th Cavalry soldiers and scouts, and the Indians fell. In the better-late-than-never department, a memorial has been erected that offers the Lakota, Northern Cheyenne, Crow, and Arikara versions of the battle. Most people are content to see Little Bighorn, but about 4.5 miles to the southeast of the main battlefield on a paved road is the **Reno-Benteen Battlefield Memorial**, now part of the 765-acre Little Bighorn Battlefield complex. The Reno-Benteen site is a tribute to soldiers who tried and failed to arrive in time to assist Custer.

Back on the Warrior Trail (US 212) heading east, you can see the stone monument to Custer on a hill as you look out the passenger side of the car. At that point, you begin to get a sense of why the natives cherish this country. There is a gentle beauty in the rolling grasslands and coulees where ponderosa pines poke out of distant ocher rimrock like many thousands of green pushpins. Painted ponies graze in pastures around the colorful array of small homes, where aging minivans, pickups, and sedans swallowed up by grasses paint a living history.

The north–south Wolf Mountains, visible on the passenger's side, serve roughly as the border between the Crow and Northern Cheyenne reservations. At **Busby** (pop. 965), just inside the Northern Cheyenne boundary, look up a hill on the south side of the highway for a stone pillar. This is the **Two Moons Monument**, a tribute to the great chief who led the Northern Cheyenne at Little Bighorn. The pillar is locked behind a chain-link fence, but you can still read the inscription and wander through a circular graveyard commemorating Northern Cheyenne killed in 1879.

At Busby, you have a choice to continue east on US 212 and the Warrior Trail, or turn south on Big Horn County Road 314 along Rosebud Creek

Indian paint ponies eye rare visitors along the Tongue River south of Ashland.

toward the Tongue River Reservoir. To stay in the battlefield flow, go 20 miles south on the paved road to **Rosebud Battlefield State Park** (406-234-0900). This is the place where a fierce battle on June 17, 1876, pitting Chief Crazy Horse's Sioux and the Northern Cheyenne against General George Crook's forces, kept the cavalry at bay long enough to prevent Crook from helping Custer at Little Bighorn eight days later. Unlike Little Bighorn, which has a visitors center and interpreters, this is a primitive area intended to retain the look and feel of 135 years ago. A short gravel road through private land leads to a kiosk describing the events and a gravel road for touring. The park also has a buffalo jump, rock cairns, and clearly visible teepee rings.

As with other great tracts of eastern Montana and northern Wyoming, the prospect of coal-bed methane gas drilling was threatening the site in 2010. Though the state owns surface rights at Rosebud, an energy company owns the valuable minerals underneath and eventually could turn the area surrounding this extraordinary historical site into an industrial zone.

Continuing southeast on the county road, the Tongue River Reservoir eventually comes into sight. This alluring 12-mile-long, caterpillar-shaped lake in the boonies, a short cast from the Wyoming border, has such extraordinary fishing that sprawling **Tongue River Reservoir State Park** (406-234-0900) annually lures 50,000 visitors, mostly boaters from Billings and Sheridan, Wyoming. There are numerous places to camp, many with full hookups, and a marina to provide all the necessary supplies for a day chasing northern pike, crappie, catfish, bass, or that eastern Montana delicacy, the walleye. The shallow and narrow reservoir has produced state records for four types of fish.

As the reservoir draws nearer, a railroad appears on the right. A spur from Sheridan, Wyoming, was built to service two huge open-pit coal mines west of the reservoir at **Decker** (pop. 96). Unless you're into seeing how some of America's thirst for energy is quenched, there is little reason to make the 6-mile trek from the state park to Decker, about a mile north of the Montana-Wyoming border.

Heading north along the lake's western shore on a well-groomed gravel road, you'll pass the dam. The road then hugs the lazy Tongue River, winding past red scoria rock and ranches north to Ashland. As you follow the river, look for deer, eagles, herons, and sandhill cranes. You'll surely notice ornate log gates for many miles—part of the vast **Diamond Cross Ranch**, which owns tens of thousands of acres east of the Tongue River (the Northern Cheyenne Reservation is on the west side).

A few miles before **Birney** (pop. 106), and on the west side of the gravel road, is a large wooden sign that creaks in the wind. "The Battle of the Butte—Jan. 8, 1877," it reads. Below it is a small commemorative stone erected by the U.S. Department of the Interior. This windswept place, nearly relegated to the dustbin of history, is on private lands, but you can try to imagine what happened here at the **Wolf Mountains Battlefield National Historic Landmark** (406-477-6035, ext. 8) and ponder its historical significance.

Seven months after Little Bighorn, Chief Crazy Horse—the hero of the nearby Battle of Rosebud—and 800 warriors tried a surprise attack on

Colonel Nelson Miles on a frigid winter morning. Miles fended off the Indians and sent them scurrying into the nearby hills. It was to be the last of the great Sioux Indian wars; within four months, all the Sioux were on distant reservations and a huge chunk of the West was open to white expansion. Given the battle's magnitude, it's surprising that there isn't more to commemorate it.

Birney is almost entirely populated by Northern Cheyenne. There isn't much here except a few well-kept homes, a school, a church, and a post office kept dust-free by a short section of pavement between shady cottonwoods. Judging by the ramshackle remnants of what must have been a mercantile, there haven't been services for a while. If you're not pressed for time, turn right on the East Fork Hanging Woman Creek Road past Poker Jim Butte for about 25 gravel miles to the **Blacks Pond Drive Route** on the Custer National Forest. In the spring and fall, this man-made pond and associated wetlands are a favorite stop for birdwatchers who admire ducks, turkeys, herons, warblers, and that Montana favorite, the Lazuli bunting. A campground and picnic area are nearby.

About six miles north of Birney, you'll have to choose between the gravel Ashland-Birney Road on the east side of the river and the paved Bureau of Indian Affairs Road 11 on the reservation on the west side. If you cross the river through a small settlement, you can continue north along the river to Ashland or save some time and drive overland to Lame Deer. We suggest staying the course to **Ashland** (pop. 464), best known for **St. Labre Indian School**, established in 1884, and **St. Labre Mission/ Cheyenne Indian Museum** (406-784-4500 Mon.–Fri.) slightly north of town. Once a three-room cabin, the school is now a campus that reflects Catholic roots and the Plains Indians lifestyle. The museum, which has a gift shop, is almost an exclusive showcase of Cheyenne history. The school and museum reflect a dedicated effort by the Northern Cheyenne to stay close to their roots; their native tongue is taught in the school and at Chief Dull Knife College in **Lame Deer** (pop. 2,028). Ashland also has a mercantile, gas station, and small diner.

Back on the Warrior Trail heading west, US 212 rises out of the Tongue River bottoms and into pretty ponderosa forest. The Northern Cheyenne economy once was dependent on logging, which is apparent in some of the small cuts and reforestation visible from the highway. You'll see signs prohibiting the shooting of prairie dogs, once considered a varmint—it still is in many circles—but now valued by many as a symbol of the plains. Look

St. Labre Mission on the outskirts of Ashland is a century-old boarding school for Crow and Northern Cheyenne.

for the telltale mounds in the fields behind barbed-wire fences. Following Alderson Creek, the highway eventually reaches Lame Deer, capital of the Northern Cheyenne nation. Don't expect your typical small-town diners and motels; they aren't here. There is a casino, expensive gas, and the Lame Deer Trading Post, aka, The Big Store. Also in town are Chief Little Wolf Hospital, a sleek, modern facility, and Chief Dull Knife College, each named after one of two chiefs who brought the Northern Cheyenne here from Oklahoma to meet up with a group led by Two Moons.

If you've got real adventurous spirit, drive about 7 miles north of Lame Deer on MT 39, cross the reservation line, perch yourself on a log stool, and have a beer and burger at the notorious **Jimtown Bar** (406-477-6459)—

after which you'll be able to boast that you've survived the toughest tavern in Montana. Don't take our word for it; the *Guinness Book of World Records* officially makes the claim. If that seems a little intimidating, go during the day; it's decidedly tamer.

Returning to US 212, the highway follows Rosebud Creek upstream about 25 miles to Busby, where the Warrior Trail tour is complete.

Best Places to Bunk

Hardin: We don't usually tout chains, but the new **Super 8 Motel** ($/$$, 406-665-1700) and **Rodeway Inn** ($, 406-665-1870) are well maintained and will suffice for a place to sleep. The Rodeway even has a waterslide open during the summer. For personality, nothing in the area tops the **Kendrick House Inn Bed & Breakfast** ($$, 406-665-3035), an immaculately manicured 1915 Edwardian boarding house with five guest rooms/suites furnished with English and French period fixtures. A garden house was made from bricks salvaged from old Fort Custer when the Smiths restored the property some 20 years ago. The breakfast, mostly the standard goods except for the lingonberry pancakes and quiche, is filling—which will keep you going on the sparsely populated trail.

Birney: Seemingly this entire vast country is at your feet with a stay at the **Lodge at Diamond Cross** ($$$$, 406-757-2220, all-inclusive), a 1930s working cattle ranch that blends the old and the new with a renovated lodge in the heart of 100,000 private acres. The land was once the camping area for the Crow and has the Tongue River snaking through it. The ranch is open year-round, can accommodate up to 13 guests, and has a three-night, three-guest minimum. A stay on the ranch gives you insight into the work and pleasures of a modern-day cattle operation.

Alternative Bunking

Camping: The **Tongue River Reservoir State Park** (406-234-0900) has every option and amenity for campers, ranging from 40 busy paved sites with electrical hookups along the reservoir to a peaceful tent-oriented campground along the river about a half mile below the dam.

Forest Service Cabins/Lookouts: (Reservations: 877-444-6777 or www.recreation.gov.) For a primitive retreat under the stars, the Custer

National Forest's **Diamond Butte Lookout** (406-784-2344, $25/sleeps four) about 40 miles east of Birney is an attractive 30-foot masonry tower. It's a pretty steep 60-yard hike from the end of the road to the lookout, but the lookout has a wagon to help haul gear. Also nearby, the 1930s **Whitetail Cabin** (406-784-2344, $25/four) is easily accessible from the road even in winter, though in snow you'll probably have to hike the length of a football field to the front door.

Best Eats

Hardin: If you have one meal in Hardin, make it at **3 Brothers Pizza & Java Co.** ($/$$, 406-665-4246, L/D Mon.–Sat.). The pizzeria, which adjoins the town's theater, is decorated with classic movie posters and has a projector with a big screen in the back of the room. The menu features paninis, pastas, burgers, homemade bread pudding, and an assortment of almost-gourmet pizzas made with their secret sauce. If you're looking for authentic diversity, **La Chalupa** ($/$$, 406-665-1175, L/D) is a pretty good Mexican restaurant and bar located in a stern-wheeler that looks as if it lost its way from the Mississippi River. But, if you find yourself in Hardin late on a Sunday night as we have, **Pizza Hut** ($/$$, 406-665-3334, L/D) will stave off hunger.

Crow Agency: The **Custer Battlefield Trading Post and Cafe** ($, 406-638-2270, B/L/D, shorter hours fall/winter) has a variety of food for the road in sit-down form or to-go. We recommend the Bear Paw (Indian fry bread stuffed with taco meat, beans, and cheese and large enough for two hungry people), potato or cowboy soup, or what they proudly call the "best Indian taco in the West." You can shop for authentic Crow and Northern Cheyenne art, souvenirs, and crafts in their remodeled gallery on the other side.

Ashland: The first restaurant you'll see on the trail after Crow Agency is the **Hitching Post Café** ($, 406-784-2779, B/L/D Mon.–Sat.), which doesn't offer anything fancy—just solid home-style cooking such as fried chicken, burgers, and a steak dinner that comes with a potato, salad, veggies, a dinner roll, and dessert for $16.95 or less, depending on the cut. And they have real, honest-to-goodness homemade pie.

TRIBAL WAR GAMES SHIFT TO NEW ARENA

Given their neighboring reservations and common histories of broken treaties and warfare with the advancing Anglo culture, you'd think the Crow and Northern Cheyenne would be kindred spirits. In fact, they have long been adversaries.

The sage plains, sculpted sandstone, and serrated mountains of the Absaroka Range have historically been Crow country. Indeed, the Absarokas are named for the tribe—*absa* meaning "beaked bird" and *roka* meaning "children"—and were the backbone of the Crow's range until the tribe was squeezed into ever-smaller reservations. The Cheyenne, meanwhile, had their genesis in the Great Lakes region and were continually pushed west by aggressive tribes, first into Minnesota and North Dakota, then to the Black Hills of South Dakota, and

Simple grave markers tell the story of a grim period in Northern Cheyenne history.

finally to the Rocky Mountains. As they moved, they shifted from sedentary to nomadic, living much like other Plains Indians. Once in the Northern Rockies, the Cheyenne frequently warred with the Crow in the Black Hills until the mid-1860s.

Not even the rapid encroachment of the Anglos could bring the two tribes together for the common good. In the most famous Indian battle in American history, the Northern Cheyenne and Sioux were allied against General George Armstrong Custer and the 7th Cavalry, which included six Crow scouts. The Crow had believed that if they helped the U.S. military they would be allowed to retain much of their historic hunting grounds. How right they are depends on your perspective. At 2.3 million acres, the Crow reservation is easily the largest of Montana's seven. But when first created in 1868, it was 15 times that size.

As punishment for the Battle of Little Bighorn, the Northern Cheyenne ultimately were marched off to Oklahoma to be with the Southern Cheyenne, where many died—especially those accustomed to the cooler climes of the north. After nearly two years living in squalor in Oklahoma, Chiefs Dull Knife and Little Wolf escaped and led a small band of Cheyenne north, where they split into two groups. Dull Knife's band was eventually imprisoned at Fort Robinson, Nebraska. Later, they escaped again, this time into what is now eastern Montana, and a reservation was finally created by presidential proclamation in 1884—in the heart of what had been Crow country.

Today, there is little evidence of the longstanding rivalry—except on the basketball floor, when Lame Deer and Lodge Grass high schools meet. It's a sight to behold: Basketball is to the Plains Indian culture what football is to America's South. Although the sheer numbers of spectators aren't in the same league, when the ball is tossed up for a breathless game of "rez ball" the intensity can rival any Friday night under the lights in Texas.

The Perfect Weekend

Check into Hardin's **Kendrick House Inn Bed & Breakfast** for the evening and stroll past the town's historic sites and murals to **3 Brothers Pizza & Java Co.** for a Greek pizza or panini. After a hearty breakfast at the Inn, stop by the **Bighorn County Historical Museum** for an hour or so. Also check out the railroad depot and various historical markers around town. Then head east on I-90 toward Crow Agency and take the Warrior Trail (US 212) exit. Allow several hours to explore the **Little Bighorn Battlefield Nation-**

al **Monument**, including a side trip to the **Reno-Benteen Battlefield Memorial** site. Returning to US 212, stop for a bite and souvenir shopping at **Custer Battlefield Trading Post and Cafe**—and buy some snacks for the road; food choices will soon become slim.

Sufficiently engrained with the area's history, you're ready to head into Crow and Northern Cheyenne Country on US 212. Stop at the **Two Moons Monument** and wander the Indian cemetery with the 1879 grave markers at the edge of Busby. Turn south on County Road 314 toward the Tongue River Reservoir and the gravel turnoff to **Rosebud Battlefield State Park**.

Back on the county road, you'll arrive at **Tongue River Reservoir State Park**. If you have camping gear or an RV, spend a night here and fish for crappie in the reservoir or rock bass in the river below the dam. Continuing north along the reservoir shore, you'll be on gravel road through **Diamond Cross Ranch** country. Just before Birney, on a slight rise, look for a butte to the left and the sign for the **Wolf Mountains Battlefield National Historic Landmark**.

Continue through Birney and cross the river onto the paved road on the Northern Cheyenne Indian Reservation. Look for herons, sandhill cranes, deer, and other wildlife along the meandering Tongue. In Ashland, stop at the grocery or **Hitching Post Café** for some refueling and take a look around the **St. Labre Indian School** and **Cheyenne Indian Museum** to see the area's history from the Indian perspective. Turn west on US 212 toward Lame Deer and return to **Crow Agency** for dinner at the **Custer Trading Post and Cafe**.

DETOUR: ONE FOR THE ROAD

The Other Warrior Trail

Billings to Crow Agency

Estimated length: 152 miles

Highlights: Sacrifice Cliff, Pictograph Cave State Park, Plenty Coups State Park, Pryor Mountains, Bighorn Canyon National Recreation Area, Bighorn Lake, Bighorn River.

Getting there: Take I-90 Exit 452 (Old US 87) just east of Billings and make an immediate right on Coburn Road.

Meandering through a sparsely populated valley, the Tongue River is one of Montana's best warm-water fisheries.

Coming from I-90, consider this loop as a memorable tune-up before hitting the Warrior Trail. Bring your camera. And your fly rod. This is a warrior trail in its own right, given that much of it traverses the Crow Reservation—and all of it crosses what was entirely Crow country, including the mysterious Pryor Mountains.

Start the drive by taking Exit 452 off I-90 on the far eastern edge of Billings and making a quick right on Coburn Road. This short side trip up the ochre-tinted limestone rimrock—probably the genesis of Yellowstone National Park's name—leads to two extraordinary pieces of Indian history: **Sacrifice Cliff** and **Pictograph Cave State Park**. First up is Sacrifice Cliff, where there are two versions of the tragedy that took place there in 1837.

Story one is that two Crow teenagers returned from an outing to find their sweethearts stricken with small pox; the grieving young warriors subsequently blinded their ponies and rode off the cliff. Story two is that as many as 16 Crows did the same after finding their entire village stricken. To reach Sacrifice Cliff, drive for a mile on Coburn Road and turn right on Canyon Trail Road and go about a half mile to the rim. Returning to Coburn Road, turn right, and head another three-plus miles to the Pictograph Cave Visitor Center.

The 500- to 9,000-year-old drawings in yawning Pictograph, Middle, and Ghost caves are faded but still visible, revealing the hopes, dreams, and fears of lost civilizations. Paths take you through box elder, sage, and grasses to sheltered rimrock, where more than 30,000 artifacts have been discovered. It is believed a perfect storm of climate conditions has enabled these paintings to survive.

Return on Coburn Road to Old US 87 (Hardin Road) near the freeway exit, and turn right. Drive about 12 miles to the junction of Pryor Creek Road and turn right toward **Pryor** (pop. 628) and **Plenty Coups State Park**, a picturesque day-use area that honors a Crow who became a chief at age 28. Plenty Coups was a great warrior, but he began farming in 1884 and continued to do so until his death in 1932. His home is now a museum that's open May 1 through September 30 or by appointment.

After leaving the park, veer west on BIA 91 across the rolling coulee country toward **St. Xavier**. Off to the right are the **Pryor Mountains**, famed today for Montana's most famous herd of wild horses and also for the so-called Little People, whom the Crow call *awwakkulé*. These mysterious peoples are said to exist somewhere between the real and spiritual world and to have provided Plenty Coups with a vision of cooperation that prevented great Crow tragedy during the whites' westward expansion. No absolute evidence of the Little People has ever been established, but the discovery of the mummified remains of numerous small individuals in the region has kept the debate alive.

As the road continues west, it forks about one-third of the way to St. Xavier, and then reconnects 20 miles later. For the more improved of the two, take the left fork, which follows Beauwais Creek. St. Xavier is the site of a Catholic mission that became a boarding school. It was here that basketball was introduced to the tribe in the late 1800s by Jesuit priests who wished to provide exercise and restore a sense of community.

At St. Xavier, you'll enter the **Bighorn Canyon National Recreation Area** and cross the Bighorn River. Turn right on MT 313 and continue to where the highway ends at **Fort Smith** (pop. 122) and Yellowtail Dam. **Bighorn Lake**, behind the dam, is one of the most popular places in the state for motorboaters, jet skiers, and water skiers. Below the dam, cold water from the bottom of the lake pours into the **Bighorn River**, creating what many believe to be the finest 13 miles of trout fishing in the world (after 13 miles, the water warms too much to support trout). Stop in any of the fly shops in Fort Smith or hire a guide; it isn't easy fishing and you'll have plenty of company despite the area's remoteness, but the right flies and technique will ensure a memorable day.

After a few hours of fishing, retrace your steps to St. Xavier on MT 313 and continue along the Bighorn River toward Hardin. About 10 miles from town, just before the Two Leggins Creek river access, you can take a shortcut east on BIA 1 over the ridge to **Crow Agency**—and the beginning of the Warrior Trail.